CONTENTS

PREFACE   v

GLOSSARY   vii

CHAPTER 1   1
Joining Oral Language and Early Literacy

CHAPTER 2   5
Explaining Terms and Fundamental Ideas

CHAPTER 3   15
Planning for Talking, Reading, and Writing a Lot

CHAPTER 4   35
Creating Learning Conditions for Progress in Talking,
Reading, and Writing

CHAPTER 5   49
Using Instructional Approaches to Teach Oral Language
and Early Literacy

CHAPTER 6   69
A Day in the Life of Ms. A. and Her 18 Preschoolers

APPENDIX A   81
Easy-to-Use Language and Literacy Assessment Tools

APPENDIX B   83
Principles of Program Evaluation

APPENDIX C   85
Daily Language and Literacy Routines for Infants
and Toddlers

REFERENCES   91

INDEX   93

Oral Language and Early Literacy in Preschool

Talking, Reading, and Writing

Kathleen A. Roskos
John Carroll University
University Heights, Ohio, USA

Patton O. Tabors
Harvard Graduate School of Education
Cambridge, Massachusetts, USA

Lisa A. Lenhart
The University of Akron
Akron, Ohio, USA

INTERNATIONAL
Reading Association
800 BARKSDALE ROAD, PO BOX 8139
NEWARK, DE 19714-8139, USA
www.reading.org

The International Reading Association attempts, through its publications, to provide a forum for a wide spectrum of opinions on reading. This policy permits divergent viewpoints without implying the endorsement of the Association.

Editorial Director, Books and Special Projects   Matthew W. Baker
Managing Editor   Shannon T. Fortner
Permissions Editor   Janet S. Parrack
Acquisitions and Communications Coordinator   Corinne M. Mooney
Associate Editor, Books and Special Projects   Sara J. Murphy
Assistant Editor   Charlene M. Nichols
Administrative Assistant   Michele Jester
Senior Editorial Assistant   Tyanna L. Collins
Production Department Manager   Iona Muscella
Supervisor, Electronic Publishing   Anette Schütz
Electronic Publishing Specialist   R. Lynn Harrison
Proofreader   Elizabeth C. Hunt

Project Editors   Matthew W. Baker and Shannon T. Fortner

Freelance Editor   Susan Hodges

Cover Design   Linda Steere

Web addresses in this book were correct as of the publication date but may have become inactive or otherwise modified since that time. If you notice a deactivated or changed Web address, please e-mail books@reading.org with the words "Website Update" in the subject line. In your message, specify the Web link, the book title, and the page number on which the link appears.

Library of Congress Cataloging-in-Publication Data
Roskos, Kathy.
   Oral language and early literacy in preschool : talking, reading, and writing / Kathleen A. Roskos.
      p. cm.
   Includes bibliographical references and index.
   ISBN 0-87207-549-4
   1. Children--Language.   2. Oral communication.   3. Reading (Early childhood)   4. Language arts (Early childhood)   I. Tabors, Patton O.   II. Lenhart, Lisa A.   III. Title.
   LB1139.L3R675 2004
   372.62'2--dc22
                                                                                                  2004010053

Much of what we learn in our lifetimes is by way of speaking, listening, reading, and writing. These are the symbolic tools that make us human; they help us to tell our stories. For this fundamental reason, it is important for preschool teachers to learn all they can about language and literacy development in young children. What they know and do makes a difference in the quality of early learning that starts off children on a language for life.

This book examines oral language and its first links to reading and writing. Its purpose is to share what we know from research about the role of oral language in children's early literacy development. Children's speaking and listening skills lead the way for their reading and writing skills, and together these language skills are the primary tools of the mind for all future learning. Please note that we use the term *oral language* to refer to speaking and listening, and the term *literacy* to refer to reading and writing. We use the word *talk* to indicate the skills of both speaking and listening.

We focus on children who are 3 and 4 years old, and who spend time in child-care, Head Start, and preschool settings. We know that all preschool educators want to ensure young children a good start in literacy, and our goal is to provide them with the knowledge they need to create high-quality language and literacy learning environments.

The book consists of six chapters. It is written particularly for preschool teachers, who must make judgments about

- what oral language skills children need to learn,
- what kinds of language and literacy experiences to provide,
- what to look for in programs and materials, and
- whether children are making progress in their use of language.

Others interested in the education and development of young children, especially policymakers, administrators, and parents, may find specific chapters informative. It is our intent and hope, however, that preschool caregivers and teachers will read the entire book to deepen and improve their early language and early literacy teaching.

Acknowledgments

We thank Adam Helbig and Abbie Wasloski for their helpful research assistance and reference searches. And we extend special thanks to Shelley Adams for graciously opening her preschool door to us and sharing her early literacy teaching practices with us.

GLOSSARY

The following glossary provides brief definitions for many of the specialized literacy terms in this book. These terms are highlighted in boldface type the first time they appear in each chapter. More detailed explanations of many of these terms and concepts can be found in chapter 2.

alphabet knowledge: The ability to name and write the 26 alphabet letters.

communication: The process of expressing and receiving ideas by means of gestures, verbal or written words, or other symbols.

decontextualized: To take something out of context.

evaluating: The process of testing and judging achievement, growth, progress, or change. This should be done via formal and informal means.

expressive language: The use of vivid and colorful language to convey feelings or attitudes. This is done orally or graphically.

language: The systematic, conventional use of sounds, signs, or written symbols in a human society for communication and self-expression (Crystal, 1992).

literacy: A written system of marks that "fixes" language in place so it can be saved. It involves reading, writing, and the thinking needed to produce and comprehend texts.

metalinguistic awareness: A conscious awareness by a language user that language is an object in itself.

monitoring: Systematically keeping track of students' progress to ensure continuous improvement.

oral language comprehension: The ability to listen and accurately reconstruct what is said on the basis of understanding.

phonological awareness: The ability to notice, think about, and work with the individual sounds in spoken words. It is also the understanding that words are made up of speech sounds or phonemes.

print knowledge: Also called *concepts of print.* Children's understandings about the functions, structure, and conventions of written language.

receptive language: The receipt of a message aurally or visually. Also, the mental store of words and phrases.

scaffolding: The process whereby a child's learning occurs in the context of full performance as adults gradually relinquish support.

screening: Evaluation to determine various abilities and learning needs.

speech: The activities of articulating and uttering sounds to produce sequences of words.

standard: Established level set to be the basic measure of achievement in a particular area.

talk: The means through which children's use of language occurs.

vocabulary: Those words known or used by a person or group.

word play: A child's manipulation of words and sounds for the purpose of pleasure, language exploration, and practice.

CHAPTER 1

Joining Oral Language and Early Literacy

Oral language is the foundation of learning to read and write. The speaking and listening skills learned in the preschool years are crucial to future reading achievement and school success. Children who do not develop strong oral language skills in the early years find it difficult to keep pace with their peers. They start to fall behind even before they start school (Snow, Burns, & Griffin, 1998).

In the early years all children need to learn to use language a lot. They need to learn how to carry on a good conversation with adults and peers. From age 3 onward, they should build a **vocabulary** store of at least 2,500 words per year. They should encounter and explore at least 2 new words each day. They need to learn how to listen on purpose.

It is through everyday experiences filled with talking, reading, and writing that children gain the oral language they need to be strong readers and learners in the future. In language-filled activity and play they learn more words, more concepts and information, and more about books and about how print works. Without this cumulative advantage, the gap in children's language widens to millions of words.

For children with too little language, learning to read and write is very hard. It is essential in these early years that all children are not only exposed to an abundance of language but also are guided to skillfully use language to be eager learners, ready readers, and budding writers.

It is not enough for children to "pick up" language on their own. It is important that they are helped to learn language in structured activities, such as shared reading, and in guided play. Children need time, resources, and ample learning opportunities to develop the oral language comprehension skills they need for school. For this to happen, adults need to be planful, purposeful, and playful (Gunnewig & McGloin, 2003) (see Figure 1).

In making plans, adults consider what children already know and can do and take steps to further their oral language comprehension. When purposeful, they set clear learning goals for children and deliberately engage them in activities that help them to explore and use language. Adults' playful language exchanges and interactions appeal to children, encouraging

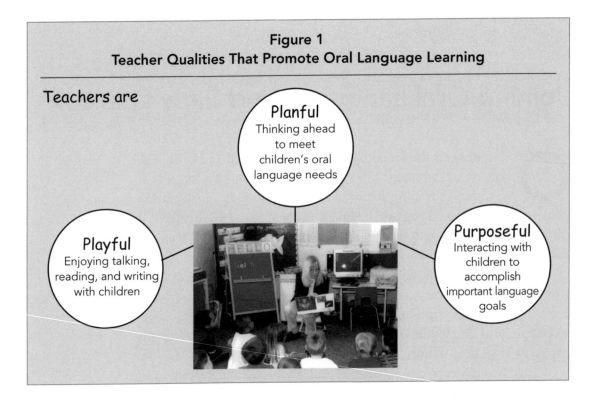

Figure 1
Teacher Qualities That Promote Oral Language Learning

Teachers are

Planful
Thinking ahead to meet children's oral language needs

Playful
Enjoying talking, reading, and writing with children

Purposeful
Interacting with children to accomplish important language goals

them to use new words and to exercise their oral language skills in different situations.

An array of instructional approaches attracts and invites children to explore, learn, and use **language**. These approaches may be used in a variety of early childhood settings from preschools to child-care centers to home-based care. They work with whole and small groups as well as individual children and include the following:

- singing and rhyming
- storytelling
- shared reading
- shared writing
- show and tell
- guided play

Adaptations for young learners with special needs and talents can easily be integrated into these instructional approaches. Throughout this book, special attention will be paid to young children learning English as a second language. Given that language is the foundation for **literacy**, it is important to think how both first- and second-language development work for young children who come from homes where English is not the primary language.

A Simple Model

Figure 2 is a simple model that shows how oral language and early literacy join together to strengthen children's school readiness. Before they go to school, children need to develop **oral language comprehension** for listening and speaking; sufficient vocabulary, **alphabet knowledge**, and **phonological awareness** to attend to the structure and sounds of language; and **print knowledge** to develop concepts about books and printed words. Preschool teachers need to plan language learning experiences that help children go beyond what they already know and can do. They need to stretch children's oral language skills by creating conditions for them to

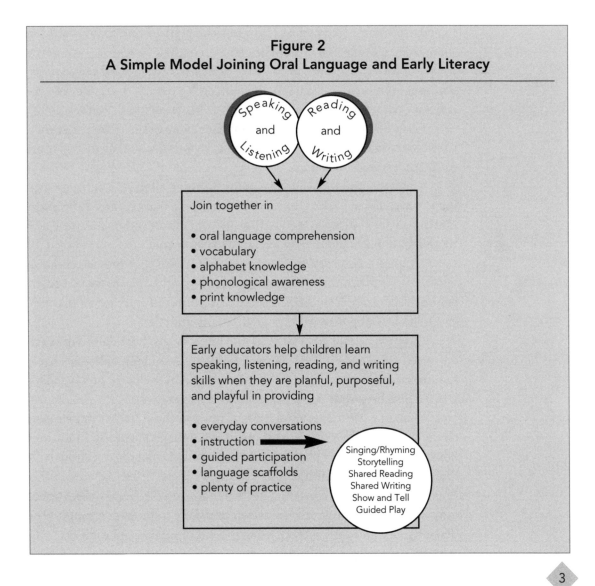

Figure 2
A Simple Model Joining Oral Language and Early Literacy

Speaking and Listening

Reading and Writing

Join together in

- oral language comprehension
- vocabulary
- alphabet knowledge
- phonological awareness
- print knowledge

Early educators help children learn speaking, listening, reading, and writing skills when they are planful, purposeful, and playful in providing

- everyday conversations
- instruction
- guided participation
- language scaffolds
- plenty of practice

Singing/Rhyming
Storytelling
Shared Reading
Shared Writing
Show and Tell
Guided Play

learn through conversations, instruction, guided participation, language scaffolds, and plenty of practice in talking, reading, and writing effectively. When teachers purposefully employ sound instructional approaches under these conditions, all children benefit.

Chapter Overviews

This book will help you use what you know and learn to make this simple model an everyday reality in your setting. Building the critical oral language foundation children need for later achievement is a giant step forward in providing high-quality early literacy education for all. Young children, especially those at risk, benefit from nurturing, robust early learning environments that expose them to rich language and many words. In these language-filled environments, young children have many wonderful opportunities to acquire the language skills they need for school (e.g., listening comprehension) and future reading achievement (e.g., sufficient vocabulary) (Bowman, Donovan, & Burns, 2001; Shonkoff & Phillips, 2000).

Chapter 2 clarifies terms and discusses some of the current research-based ideas that link oral language and early literacy so that we can more easily understand each area.

Chapter 3 provides suggestions for planning effective language learning experiences and assessing children's progress. It also offers some information about how to make the best use of resources, such as time and materials, to boost children's language development.

Chapter 4 describes how to create conditions that provide children with many opportunities to develop and advance their language and emergent literacy skills. It outlines the basic structures of interaction that pull children's learning forward in shared activity and play.

Chapter 5 describes instructional approaches. It explains why each approach is important as a language and literacy builder, outlines what is required to implement it, and illustrates what it looks like in practice. This chapter also lists some appropriate materials to use.

Chapter 6 gives an example of how one preschool teacher implements a language-rich program that joins oral language and early literacy. It demonstrates that with planning, purpose, and play, adults can equip children with a language for life.

The appendixes contain a list of language and literacy assessment tools, principles of program evaluation, and daily routines that support the oral language and early literacy development of infants and toddlers.

CHAPTER 2

Explaining Terms and Fundamental Ideas

How children develop language is a topic of intense study. Over decades, much has been learned about this remarkable process, far more than we could ever discuss in one small book. Familiarity with a few basic terms and ideas about language and early literacy will help you plan stimulating oral language experiences and communicate more clearly with both educators and children.

Nearly all the terms and concepts presented here are useful when thinking about any language system, not just English. Two exceptions apply: (1) Not all languages have a written form, and (2) some languages that are written do not use an alphabet.

All languages start with a group of sounds that must be learned and used by the infants in the families where that language is spoken. All languages have words that are made up of a variety of those sounds. And all conversation in all languages is made up of a group of words put together to express an idea. Communication in any language involves expressing and receiving ideas in a way that is understandable for all the people involved in the communication.

For young children who come from homes where English is not the primary language, all of these skills will have been developed in their home language. They will have learned the sounds of their language, the words of their language, and how to put words together to form ideas. So these young children will already know a great deal about how language works. They will bring those skills to the task of learning a new language. But it is important to remember that these children will need to start again with the sounds of their new language, with the words of their new language, and with the rules about how conversation works in their new language. This is a very big job for young children.

A Few Key Terms

The following definitions are a useful introduction to a few foundational concepts about language and early literacy that will be discussed later in the book. Some of these definitions expand on terms introduced in the Glossary.

Alphabet Knowledge

Alphabet knowledge is the ability to name and write the 26 alphabet letters. Alphabet letters are the building blocks of our writing system. The name of an alphabet letter (e.g., *M*) often gives a clue to its sound, which is valuable information for emerging readers and writers. Children should know about 10 alphabet letters, including those in their own first name, before they enter kindergarten (U.S. Department of Health and Human Services, 2003).

Communication

Communication is the process of expressing and receiving ideas. It involves the exchange of meaning between people. Ideas can be sent and received in different ways, such as by gestures, pictures, and movements. Language is the richest and most versatile means of communication.

Language

Language is a verbal system. It consists of words and rules for organizing words and changing them. From birth, children are exposed to the language of their families; they learn the words their families use. They develop their own grammar style to combine words (e.g., *Me want juice.*) and change words (e.g., *I goed with grandma.*). By age 4 most children have grasped the grammar rules of their language. They increasingly use language for social exchanges, requests, finding out, telling, and play. (See Figure 3 for an overview of language milestones.)

Figure 3
Milestones in Language Development

Age	Language Milestone
3 months	Makes cooing sounds
11 months	Uses multiple-syllable babbling (*mama, dada, baba*)
16 months	Uses some words besides *mama* and *dada*
23 months	Can form two-word sentences
34 months	Uses prepositions; carries on a conversation
47 months	Can be understood by strangers most of the time

Adapted from Vukelich, Christie, & Enz (2002)

Literacy

Literacy is a written system of marks that fixes language in place so it can be saved. It involves the reading, writing, and thinking needed to produce and comprehend texts. Spelling and punctuation rules govern our writing system and must be learned if one is to become literate. Depending on their family literacy environments, children begin forming ideas about books and print in infancy. By 2 years of age, they may pretend to read to dolls, stuffed animals, or themselves. And by age 4, many can read environmental print, their own name, and a few common words (e.g. *hello* or *exit*). In kindergarten, children start to read predictable books and spell simple words. By age 8, most children are expected to read and write at a third-grade level (Snow, Burns, & Griffin, 1998). (See Figure 4 for an overview of early stages of reading development.)

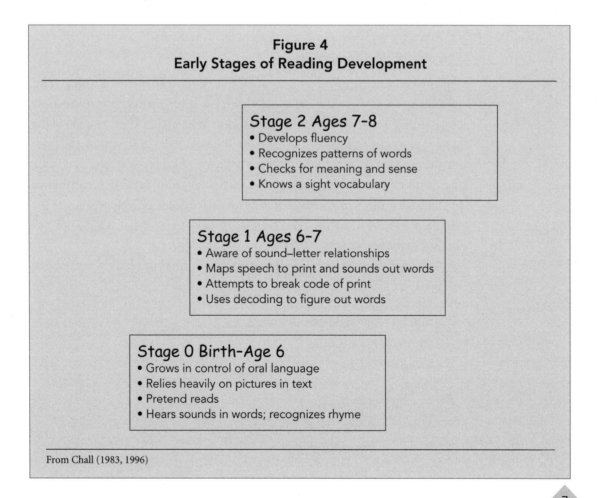

Figure 4
Early Stages of Reading Development

Stage 2 Ages 7–8
- Develops fluency
- Recognizes patterns of words
- Checks for meaning and sense
- Knows a sight vocabulary

Stage 1 Ages 6–7
- Aware of sound–letter relationships
- Maps speech to print and sounds out words
- Attempts to break code of print
- Uses decoding to figure out words

Stage 0 Birth–Age 6
- Grows in control of oral language
- Relies heavily on pictures in text
- Pretend reads
- Hears sounds in words; recognizes rhyme

From Chall (1983, 1996)

Oral Language Comprehension

Oral language comprehension is the ability to listen and respond with understanding. To comprehend oral language, children need to pay attention and listen on purpose. They need to accurately and quickly recognize the words they hear. And at the same time, they need to connect the new information they hear with what they already know. From this, children build meanings that indicate they are comprehending ideas, as shown by what they do and say. Children's oral language comprehension abilities improve when they are read to, asked interesting questions, given clear explanations, and encouraged to express their ideas. Read-alouds are especially beneficial because while listening to stories and information books, children also learn book language, book structure, new concepts, and new vocabulary. These opportunities not only build the skill of listening with understanding but also expand children's background knowledge and the amount of words they can use to talk about experiences.

Phonological Awareness

This involves hearing the sounds of language apart from its meaning. This mental work is difficult for most children. It requires them to become consciously aware of the structure of language, rather than simply using language to communicate. They need to learn how to listen on purpose for the number of words in sentences (e.g., *We / had / eggs / for / breakfast.*), the number of syllables in words (e.g., *fish-er-man*), and the number of individual sounds in words (e.g., /h/ /a/ /t/). Phonological awareness is a strong predictor of future reading success and an essential skill for phonics and spelling (Stanovich, 2000).

The following exchange offers an example of phonological awareness:

• • • • • • • • • • • • • • •

Adult:	I'm thinking of a word that begins with /m/ and rhymes with *fan*.
Children:	Man!
Adult:	Man. That's right. When you put /m/ and /an/ together you get *man*.
Adult:	Now I'm thinking of a word that begins with /s/ and rhymes with *bun*.
Children:	Sun!

Adult:	How about a word that begins with /f/ and rhymes with *meet*?
Children:	Feet!

• • • • • • • • • • • • • • • •

Speech

Speech refers to the activities of articulating and uttering sounds to pro-duce sequences of words. Barring hearing loss, all children gradually learn to use speech on purpose to express meaning as they talk. Speech devel-ops in an orderly and predictable progression, from babble to single words to two or three word utterances and finally to complex sentences. The rate of development, however, varies tremendously in individual children. Some children are early talkers while others are late talkers. Put another way, some like to "schmooze," tending to be more social, while others are too busy or absorbed in activities to talk.

Talk

Talk is the means through which children's use of language occurs. Through talk with others, children build their practical knowledge of lan-guage—the verbal system. They learn to talk by talking. This is how they learn new words and gain mastery of language rules. Children's language knowledge (words and rules), gained through talking, becomes the basis for developing essential reading and writing skills. How much and how well children can use language is evident in their talk.

The following is a sample of children's language:

• • • • • • • • • • • • • • • •

Suspicious Stuff

Lauren and Lesley, twin girls about 4 years old, are whispering secre-tively to one another as we run errands between home, school, and grocery store. They are gathering up small objects along the way. They snatch a paper clip. "This is 'suspicious stuff,'" one whispers to the other. They spot a knot of rubber bands—and this, too, is "sus-picious stuff." Next a few crumpled scraps of paper are added to the collection. Lauren spies a shiny, blue sequin. "Very suspicious stuff," she tells Lesley. "Would an envelope help," I ask, "to hold your 'stuff'?" And Lesley replies that it "surely" would and adds, in a hushed tone, "but make it say 'suspicious stuff.'"

• • • • • • • • • • • • • • • •

Vocabulary

Vocabulary is used to describe the store of words children know. It is organized into two large types: (1) expressive vocabulary, words children can use to express themselves, and (2) receptive vocabulary, words they can understand when heard in context. Generally children's receptive vocabulary (listening) is larger than their expressive vocabulary (speaking). The average preschooler knows about 5,000 words and by the end of high school will have an estimated vocabulary size of about 60,000 words (Bloom, 2000). Vocabulary is learned gradually over many encounters with a new word again and again. Children benefit from language-rich environments that expose them to many new words used many different times in many different ways.

Three Fundamental Concepts

Before children are readers and writers, they are speakers and listeners. Progressing from saying words to reading and writing them demands a big shift in children's thinking. They must become conceptually aware that there is a code to be deciphered and that it is different from speech. Reading print is more than understanding speech written down.

The following concepts explain how oral language and literacy are alike and different (see Figure 5 for an outline of Halliday's [1977] functions of language and Figure 6 for five functions of early literacy [Neuman & Roskos, 1989]). When you know more about the relationship between speech and print you can help young children make the mental shift from the more familiar world of talking to the less familiar one of reading and writing.

Concept 1: Talk and Print Are Alike

Talking, reading, and writing are interrelated processes. All three involve using words to "stand for" or represent persons, objects, and events in the world. Each draws from the other in real experience. Children speak and listen, they listen to reading, they read what they write, and so on. These overlapping processes are "tools of the mind" that children can use to get things done. Talking, reading, and writing join together to build children's knowledge about the world and about words. At the starting line of learn-

Figure 5
Language Functions

Language Functions That Children Learn

Instrumental Function	"I want"	to communicate desires, wishes
Regulatory Function	"Do as I say"	to control behaviors of others
Interactional Function	"Me and you"	to manage the social environment
Personal Function	"Here I come"	to express self, feelings
Heuristic Function	"Tell me why"	to ask about the world
Imaginative Function	"Let's pretend"	to create new worlds

From Halliday (1977)

Figure 6
Early Literacy Functions

Literacy Functions That Children Demonstrate

Exploratory Function	"How does it work?"	to experiment with print
Interactional Function	"Between you and me"	to share information
Personal Function	"For me"	to claim ownership
Authenticating Function	"To legitimate"	to act grown up
Transactional Function	"Between me and text"	to label; to make meaning

From Neuman & Roskos (1989)

ing to read and write, children rely on their considerable speech experiences to help them with print experiences.

Concept 2: Talk and Print Are Different

There are important differences between spoken and written language that make learning to read harder than learning to talk. Why? There are two main reasons. One, print is a code for speech that relies on the manipulation of a set of symbols (26 alphabet letters). And, because it is a code, children need to be taught how to decode print before they can say it. This extra step requires extra mental effort. Adults must help children find the relationship between print symbols and speech sounds and help them make the effort to remember. And two, print is **decontextualized**: It does not have the real-time qualities of speech such as tone, pitch, expression, and rhythm that signal meaning. Before they go to school, children experience mostly talking that occurs in rich contexts. When a mother says to her 4-year-old son, "Put on your pajamas. It's time for bed," there is an abundance of real cues to help him know what this means. Children interact with peers in rich, meaningful, social play contexts. Even speech on television and computer games has many sensory clues as to what the talk refers to and why a person is talking.

Print is different. It is silent and still. Its meaning must be unbundled from the print itself by an active mind. This, too, requires extra mental effort to "pick out" the meaning from the words alone. Adults must show children how to think with print in order to make it meaningful. This is why reading to and with children is so powerful—because it shows them how to do what they need to do to comprehend the print code.

Concept 3: Speaking, Listening, Reading, and Writing Share Skills

Fortunately concepts and skills learned for oral language are shared with literacy and vice versa. Here are a few of the most essential.

Making Predictions.   This is the ability to use context to choose the appropriate language. At a friend's birthday party, children remember to say "Happy Birthday" because the setting reminds them of the event. They chime in, chanting "Chicka, chicka, boom, boom" as you read a popular storybook to them. Similarly, they use the skill of prediction to guess what a printed word might be when they hear its beginning sound or connect visual cues with the meaning (e.g., the tail at the end of *pig*).

Asking and Answering Questions.   In oral language, questions are signs of seeking, noticing, and incorporating new and more complex experiences into prior experiences. They signal what's going on in children's minds while invisible mental schemas are busily being organized and built. Questions indicate children's skill in monitoring comprehension; through their questions, we can see that children are "following along" and "getting it" whether it be a conversation, a book reading, a play episode, or a table activity. Questioning is a vital skill in speaking and listening as well as in reading and writing.

Telling and Retelling.   These expressive verbal skills exercise children's use of language to tell, recount, report, explain, and pretend. Children need many opportunities to practice their expressive language skills so that they learn to include the details. In speaking, listening, reading, and writing, details matter. Attention to detail increases the length of sentences, the size of vocabulary, and the grammatical complexity of the talk. Details also enlarge the child's fund of background knowledge.

Sense of Story.   Children's personal stories about their real experiences indicate their storytelling abilities. Stories are one way they learn to represent their experience. Stories provide an organizer for holding an experience in mind and replaying it at will. Storytelling is also the forerunner of grasping the story structures found in literature. Children's oral storytelling abilities lay the foundation for using story elements to comprehend stories in books.

Phonological Awareness.   As a skill, phonological awareness places special demands on children's abilities to self-regulate their thinking and actions. They must *listen for* specific words or sounds; *listen to* words and sounds carefully in order to manipulate them; and *listen with* the intention to act for a specific purpose, such as clapping for each word heard in a sentence, tapping for each sound heard in a word, completing a rhyme, singing and clapping in rhythm, and so on. Learning to read and write depends heavily on phonemic awareness, which is the basis of matching sounds to printed letters and decoding printed words.

You can think of making predictions, asking and answering questions, telling and retelling, sense of story, and phonological awareness as "crossover skills" because they cross over children's talking, reading, and writing to the benefit of all three. Knowing about these skills will help you be more effective and more efficient as you plan lively language experiences for the eager talkers and emerging readers and writers in your setting.

The purpose of this chapter was to familiarize you with fundamental concepts in language and early literacy by introducing key terms and developmental overviews in language and literacy. How children talk and use print were compared and contrasted to deepen your understanding of oral language and the role it plays in learning to read and write.

CHAPTER 3

Planning for Talking, Reading, and Writing a Lot

A quality setting that unites oral language and early literacy learning does not just happen. It takes planning, action, good management, and an eye to continuous improvement. Planning includes assessment that provides a clear picture of what children in your setting can already do with their speaking, listening, reading, and writing abilities and what they need to accomplish in both the long and short terms. It involves making good use of resources, such as time, materials, and routines, to get the best results. Planning is the foundation of intentional teaching for integrating oral language and early literacy learning that helps children make progress.

Long-Term Planning

Long-term planning describes the goals and objectives for children's **language** learning over the entire time of your program. To plan effectively, you need to be familiar with the early learning standards in language and literacy adopted by professional organizations (e.g., *Learning to Read and Write: Developmentally Appropriate Practices for Young Children* [International Reading Association & National Association for the Education of Young Children, 1998]), early childhood programs (e.g., Head Start Child Outcomes Framework [U.S. Department of Health and Human Services, 2003]), or your state department of education. (See Figure 7 for sources of early learning standards.)

These standards are valid statements of expectations in oral language and literacy that young children should achieve before kindergarten. If you have English-language learners in your classroom, look carefully for information about how these standards are to be applied to them.

We agree, for example, that all children should use an increasingly complex and varied vocabulary across the preschool years. This is an important oral language goal in your long-term planning. But it is too general for guiding practical activity. You will need to break down this goal into more manageable objectives (see Figure 8). Depending on your setting, this

---

Figure 7
Sources of Early Learning Standards in Language and Literacy

Head Start Child Outcomes Framework: www.hsnrc.org/CDI/outcontent.cfm

McREL "A Framework for Early Literacy Instruction: Aligning Standards to Developmental Accomplishments and Student Behaviors": www.mcrel.org/topics/productDetail.asp?topicsID=8&productID=7

The Department of Education in Your State: For example, the Ohio Early Learning Content Standards: www.ode.state.oh.us/ece/Standards1

Figure 8
An Oral Language Goal Broken Down to Objectives

Goal: Children will stay on and extend a topic of conversation.

	Objectives
September	Help children use their language to join in conversations. Draw their attention to the listener's needs.
October	Encourage contributions to a conversation. Support use of social conventions, such as "excuse me," "please," and "thank you."
November	Help children coordinate gesture and tone of voice to convey meaning. Encourage them to add details and feedback information.

You should develop objectives for each essential skill area: oral language comprehension, vocabulary, alphabet knowledge, phonological awareness, and print knowledge. While you will provide continuous support for language and early literacy in a variety of ways, it is helpful to focus on a few key objectives for a period of time.

---

may be every few months, monthly, or weekly. Most preschool standards are accompanied by performance indicators that detail exactly what children should know and be able to do. This makes determining objectives for oral language and early literacy instruction much easier.

Short-Term Planning

Short-term planning describes the key activities you will implement in order to meet the goals and objectives that develop children's language and literacy concepts, skills, and habits. It results in your weekly planner, which should be clear and concise, including enough details so that someone else could follow it if necessary, and short enough to fit on one piece of paper (see Figure 9). Weekly plans should reflect your long-term plan. Activities you plan each week should support children's reaching established early learning standards in language and literacy. They should address objectives or performance indicators that are directly linked to larger goals or expectations. Your weekly plans should also guide your daily planning to ensure consistency in children's language and literacy experiences. When long- and short-term plans are consistent with one another, opportunity for children to gain essential language and literacy skills is greatly increased.

Figure 9
A Few Days From a Weekly Planner

Day	Focus on...	Activities
Monday	Listening attentively to a story (OLC) Drawing attention to listener's needs (OLC) Learning construction-related new words (V)	1. Enjoying the story *Knock It Down, Build It Up!* 2. Discussing construction-related photos in small group 3. Helping children plan their own construction company for dramatic play
Tuesday	Helping to tell a story (OLC) Listening and taking turns (OLC, V) Exploring print and sounds (AK, PA, PK)	1. Taking a picture walk of *Knock It Down, Build It Up!* (Children tell the story) 2. Discussing and exploring tools for building in small group 3. Helping children plan the construction company play center
Wednesday	Remembering story sequence (OLC) Using new "construction" words (V) Recognizing rhyming words (PA)	1. Reviewing sequence of *Knock It Down, Build It Up!* 2. Exploring rhyming words 3. Making a scrapbook of buildings in our neighborhood 4. Setting up the play center

OLC = Oral language comprehension
V = Vocabulary
AK = Alphabet knowledge
PA = Phonological awareness
PK = Print knowledge

Assessment Informs Planning

Assessment is an integral part of intentional teaching and the basis of continuous improvement. It is a data-gathering process with the primary aim of determining what children can and cannot yet do. This information informs your instructional planning and program decision making. It helps you to build the best connections between oral language and early literacy.

Assessment should occur regularly to determine children's needs, inform planning, and guide purposeful instruction. A wide variety of assessment tools is available to screen, monitor, and evaluate children's developmental progress in language and early literacy. You should become familiar with some of the easier-to-use assessment tools and be prepared to discuss the results with others. (See Appendix A for a list of easy-to-use assessments.)

If you have English-language learners in your classroom, you should become familiar with the stages of second-language development that researchers have noted for these children. Your assessment of their progress will depend on your knowing what to expect.

Second-Language Development

Researchers have outlined the following sequence of second-language development of young children (McLaughlin, Blanchard, & Osanai, 1995). Of course, as with all developmental processes, there are variations in how children approach this process and how long it will take for them to go through these stages. But it is clearly important to have these stages in mind when assessing English-language learners' language use in your classroom.

- First, the child uses the home language. When everyone around the child is speaking a different language, there are only two options—(1) to speak the language they already know or (2) to stop speaking entirely. Many children, but not all, follow the first option for some period of time (Saville-Troike, 1987). This, of course, leads to increasing frustration, and eventually children give up trying to make others understand their language.

- The second stage is the nonverbal period. After children abandon the attempt to communicate in their first language, they enter a period in which they do not talk at all. This can last for some time, or it can be a brief phase. Although they do not talk during this time, children attempt to communicate nonverbally to get help from adults or to obtain objects. Furthermore, this is a period during which children begin actively to "crack the code" of the second language. Saville-Troike (1987) noted that children will rehearse the target language by repeating what other speakers say in a low voice and by playing with the sounds of the new language.

- The next stage occurs when the child is ready to go public with the new language. There are two characteristics to this speech—it is telegraphic and it involves the use of formulas. Telegraphic speech is common in early monolingual language development and involves the use of a few content words without function words or morphological markers. For example, a young child learning to speak English may say "put paper" to convey the meaning "I want to put the paper on the table." Formulaic speech refers to the use of unanalyzed chunks of words or routine phrases that are repetitions of what the child hears. Children use such prefabricated chunks long before they have any understanding of what they mean (Wong Fillmore, 1976).

- Eventually, the child reaches the stage of productive language use. At this point the child is able to go beyond short telegraphic utterances and memorized chunks. Initially, children may form new utterances by using formulaic patterns such as "I wanna" with names for objects. In time, the child begins to demonstrate an understanding of the syntactic system of the language. Children gradually unpackage their formulas and apply newly acquired grammar rules to develop productive control over the language.

Screening

Set aside time during the first few weeks of your program to quickly determine children's speaking and listening abilities as well as their emerging literacy skills. We suggest that you use a formal screening tool for this purpose along with informal observations of children as they work and play together. Meet with each child in a quiet place to conduct the screening. At other times during the day, use an informal checklist like that in Figure 10 to document children's use of language and their early literacy behaviors. This dual approach is well worth your time and effort because it provides a rich baseline of information for planning that leads to more purposeful language and literacy experiences.

Figure 10
Oral Language Checklist

Key: (+) Consistently (✓) Sometimes (–) Not yet

Child Observed: _____

Observer: _____

Date	Observational Setting			Comments
	Large Group	Small Group	Individual	
Speaking				
Responds when spoken to				
Takes turns speaking				
Participates in group discussions				
Recalls and recites songs and fingerplays				
Speaks clearly				
Speaks in complete sentences				
Initiates conversations				
Asks questions				
Tells a personal story				
Uses appropriate sentence structure (word order, pronouns, verbs)				
Listening				
Listens to rhymes, songs, and stories with interest				
Listens to speaker in conversations				
Follows single-step direction				
Follows multiple-step directions				
Vocabulary				
Plays with words				
Links new words to what is already known about a topic				
Uses new words appropriately in conversation and discussion				

From *Doors to Discovery Assessment Handbook*. Copyright © 2002 Wright Group/McGraw-Hill. Reprinted with permission.

Monitoring

For continuous improvement, it is important to keep track of children's progress while they are in your program. This will allow you to determine if children are developing adequately or need more help to thrive. We recommend that you assemble a set of short speaking, listening, reading, and writing activities that coincide with your curriculum for the purpose of tracking children's progress. Your set of assessment activities should tap the critical areas of **oral language comprehension, vocabulary, alphabet knowledge, phonological awareness,** and **print knowledge.** Establish a time each week to check on children's progress either in small groups or individually. For example, you might ask children to write their first names in their own First Name Book every week so you can see at a glance how well individual children are doing with this skill. At the same time you can note the alphabet letters they start to recognize in their own names. A sample Assessment Chart is provided in Figure 11. Note that assessment activities can be theme related and easily woven into the typical structure of the day.

Evaluating

Assessment includes evaluation. It is necessary to find out if your program is effective and children are achieving worthy goals in language and literacy. This can be done in at least two ways. Your program may already use a commercial test to determine children's achievement in key areas of

Figure 11
Assessment Chart

Theme: _____   Date: _____

Names	Oral Language • Describes experience • Uses in play	Vocabulary • Names • Classifies • Uses new words	Alphabet • Names letters • Forms letters	Phonological Awareness • Identifies rhymes • Claps syllables	Print Knowledge • Orients to book • Reads some words • Chimes in

language and early literacy upon program completion, such as the *Peabody Picture Vocabulary Test* (Dunn, Dunn, Robertson, & Eisenberg, 1997). Check for a good match between your program goals and what the test measures before making judgments about program effectiveness.

If no end-of-program assessment is required in your setting, you can repeat the screening, using the formal tool along with your informal observations as backup, to make judgments about how well children are doing and overall program quality. Using either of these approaches, results should be used to describe where children presently are in their skill development and to make improvements in your program. One of the most powerful uses of evaluation is to improve program quality for children's higher achievement in essential speaking, listening, reading, and writing skills. (For further discussion, see the Principles of Program Evaluation in Appendix B.)

Developing a Long-Term Plan for Language and Literacy Learning

Assessment informs planning, and early learning standards lead the way for both. By using assessment information and standards, you are prepared to develop a long-term plan that outlines excellent oral language and literacy experiences for young children. Consider the key areas of oral language comprehension, vocabulary, alphabet knowledge, phonological awareness, and print knowledge. Think about

- the different uses of language children will need to learn for social interaction, for early literacy, and thinking;
- what speaking and listening skills you will develop in children;
- what you will cover in vocabulary;
- what you will teach about recognizing and writing alphabet letters; and
- which phonological awareness skills you will teach.

Using Learning Trajectories

Expectations or early learning standards reflect our best judgment, informed by research and experience, of what children should accomplish in language and literacy at or about a certain age. Expectations are plotted along learning trajectories that show what we should expect of children as they grow older. Preschool learning trajectories for oral language comprehension, vocabulary, alphabet knowledge, phonological awareness, and print knowledge are illustrated in Figure 12. In developing your long-range

Figure 12
Learning Trajectories

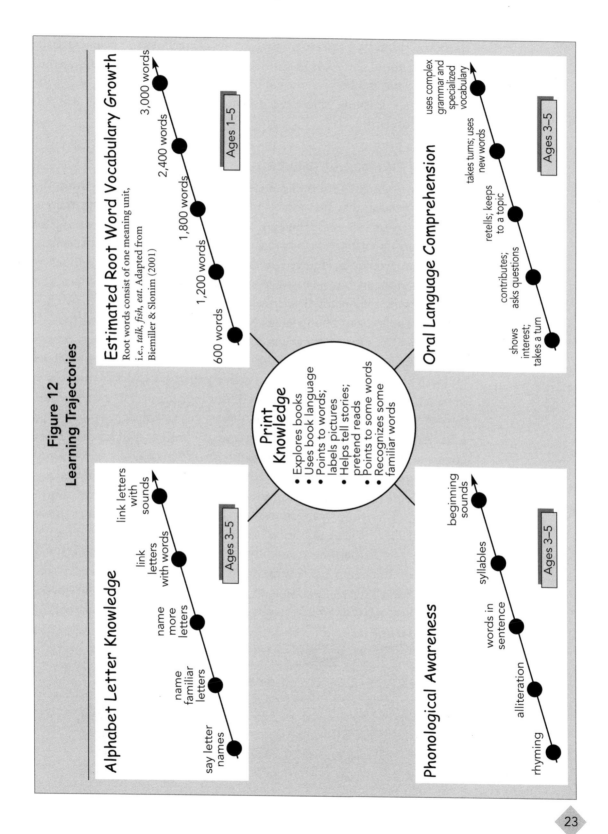

Estimated Root Word Vocabulary Growth

Root words consist of one meaning unit, i.e., *talk, fish, eat.* Adapted from Biemiller & Slonim (2001)

- 600 words
- 1,200 words
- 1,800 words
- 2,400 words
- 3,000 words

Ages 1–5

Alphabet Letter Knowledge

- say letter names
- name familiar letters
- name more letters
- link letters with words
- link letters with sounds

Ages 3–5

Print Knowledge
- Explores books
- Uses book language
- Points to words; labels pictures
- Helps tell stories; pretend reads
- Points to some words
- Recognizes some familiar words

Oral Language Comprehension

- shows interest; takes a turn
- contributes; asks questions
- retells; keeps to a topic
- takes turns; uses new words
- uses complex grammar and specialized vocabulary

Ages 3–5

Phonological Awareness

- rhyming
- alliteration
- words in sentence
- syllables
- beginning sounds

Ages 3–5

plan, you should use research-based learning trajectories to help you make decisions about the goals and objectives of your program. You need to compare what children can do, gathered from your assessments, to benchmarks on the learning trajectories and decide on experiences that will pull children forward.

Using Thematic Organizers

Thematic organizers collect language and literacy experiences around a sound set of ideas that are valuable to explore for both adults and children. These organizers also ease the hard work of developing a long-term plan by breaking down a task into manageable chunks. Preschool teachers have long organized young children's learning experiences around themes or units. But, to truly boost language and literacy skills for all children, not just any theme will do. You need to select themes that deliberately build children's world and word knowledge. Not just ordinary themes, such as "All About Me" or "Our Furry Friends," but extraordinary themes, such as "Fossils," "Gardens and Gardening," or "Color and Light," that introduce children to the powerful ideas of science, mathematics, social studies, art, and literature are needed. (See Figure 13 for four features of an extraordinary theme.) Such themes go beyond day-to-day knowledge and language to include rare vocabulary (not just everyday words) and all kinds of book language from stories to informational texts. When carefully selected and sequenced, themes provide cumulative and repeated opportunities to develop children's oral language comprehension, vocabulary, and print awareness. English-language learners also can benefit from these themes in the classroom. But it will be important to remember to present information in visual as well as verbal formats so English-language learners can understand the topic of discussion. Presenting vocabulary with both visual and verbal cues will help all the children start to understand and use their new words.

Figure 13
Features of an Extraordinary Theme

- **Content rich:** Children will gain world knowledge.
- **Engaging:** Children will find the topic interesting.
- **Enduring:** Children will remember important ideas and facts.
- **Thoughtful:** Children will learn to think and question.

Putting the Long-Term Plan Into Action: The Weekly Planner

The weekly planner is a practical tool that serves as a bridge between the daily lesson and the long-term plan. The planner helps preschool teachers to coordinate learning activities on a weekly basis so that they fit together and join to build children's language and literacy skills. The day-to-day purpose is to unite oral language and early literacy learning to the advantage of both. When children improve their oral language comprehension, this lays the foundation for better reading comprehension later on. When they are guided to attend to specific sounds in language, children become better listeners who can get the most out of conversations and book reading experiences. As they interact with different texts, children encounter new words that increase the vocabulary they can bring to reading and writing.

When you make your weekly plan, you need to consider which speaking, listening, reading, and writing skills will be carefully guided and which ones will be less catered to in the round of daily activities for that week. You should think about what you will teach to the whole group of children, to small groups, and to individuals and ensure that children have ample time to explore new language uses, words, and print skills on their own. And you need to consider the instructional approaches you will use to expose children to language and literacy content and skills. (Instructional approaches are described in chapter 5.) For rich language use to occur, you need to bring these important considerations to mind as you prepare your plan for the week.

Rhythm of the Day

While organizing your weekly planner you may want to think about how speaking, listening, reading, and writing skills can become well integrated into the rhythm of the day.

Greeting Time. In addition to modeling and exchanging social courtesies that encourage speaking and listening, greeting time is an ideal opportunity for children to practice their print skills. One good idea is to have children "Sign In" by writing their first names (or making their mark) on chart paper at an easel (see Figure 14 for a sign-in procedure).

Activity Time. Much of activity time (play and table work) should be filled with language as children play together and work on small projects

Figure 14
The Sign-In Procedure

Purpose: Children write their first names as a daily attendance activity.

Benefit: Children learn the alphabet letters in their own name.

Procedure:
1. Prepare a Sign-In sheet with the names of four or five children on each page.
2. Tell the children, "I need your help to keep daily attendance. Every day when you arrive, you will sign in. You will put your name on this Sign-In sheet. Here's what you do. Find your name on the Sign-In sheet. Write your name in the box next to it as best as you can. This is your signature. When you sign in, we all know you are here with us today."
3. Show the children how to follow the steps: *Arrive, Go to the Sign-In Spot, Find Your Name on the Sheet, Sign In.*
4. Maintain the sign-in sheets in a folder to note children's progress in name writing.

Adapted from McGee & Richgels (2003)

with adults. These are opportune times for conversation, discussion, and role-play. You should also deliberately use these times for modeling how to ask questions to clarify or gain information or analyze and explore ideas, and to prompt children to find solutions to questions (*Why do our shadows become longer or shorter? What does the architect do?*). For English-language learners you may want to model how children can ask for help from others (e.g., Say to Sammy, "May I have some play dough?").

Circle Time. Beyond shared reading and sharing time, consider using circle time for developing children's storytelling abilities and listening comprehension. Tell stories to children drawn from your own childhood memories. Assist children in having wonderful ideas about stories they can tell. Help them prepare. Invite them to share their own stories with the group. A storytelling program gives children practice in speaking in front of an audience, develops their sense of story, exercises their use of **decontextualized** speech, and is exciting for them. These activities may be particularly challenging for English-language learners. Make sure that they are ready to participate actively in these events. If they are not ready, find another activity that they can be part of that will let them show off their growing language competence.

Outdoor Time. Use outdoor time for extending language and **literacy** experiences by modeling new games children can play and for assisting children in using language effectively to negotiate the rules and procedures for play and to resolve conflicts. On neighborhood outings with the children, point out environmental print that is present on stores and businesses, posters and storefront advertisements, traffic signs, and so on. Carry information from these literacy walks back to your settings, incorporating it into your lessons and play centers.

Essentials in the Daily Plan

Your daily plan is your guide to action in the busy, unpredictable world of your setting. It helps you to organize and manage your time with children to their benefit as learners. Time well spent involves you in working with the whole group, working with small groups, and having children play well independently. When working with the whole group you should include some direct teaching and demonstrating of speaking, listening, reading, and writing skills. For example, you might role-play language and appropriate behavior for buying or selling in the class Grocery Store. Plan to spend about 10–15 minutes each day teaching specific concepts and skills for talking, reading, and writing with a whole group of preschoolers.

You should group children in pairs or small groups (with three or four members) for instructional purposes. Children make better progress in these situations because they have more chances to use and attend to language and print under the guidance of an adult. There are two different types of groups that work well—heterogeneous groups and homogeneous groups. Heterogeneous groups are made up of children with different ability levels; homogeneous groups gather together children with similar strengths and weaknesses. Neither type of group should be seen as permanent, but rather as flexible, with children leaving and joining different groups depending on the instructional purpose. For example, you might gather one or two heterogeneous groups together to make a sand clock in the whole-class exploration of time and timekeepers. Later homogeneous groups of children may be formed for board games and puzzles that develop alphabet letter knowledge. This allows you to pitch your instruction so that it is neither too hard nor too easy for any one child in the group. If you have English-language learners in your classroom, consider how you can alternate their experiences, sometimes having them work with children who are more fluent in English, and sometimes having them work in groups with other English-language learners, so that you can tailor instruction to their needs.

One big concern for preschool teachers is what the rest of the children will be doing that is productive for them when you are working with small groups or pairs. They should be playing with one another in inviting, print-rich settings that advance their talk, reading, and writing. For this, you need to make sure that play settings stimulate pretending, complex themes, and complex roles. You need to allow sufficient time for uninterrupted play, at least 30–40 minutes daily. And you need to prepare children for play by helping them make a plan for their play, periodically checking in on their progress, and coaching them on the spot when they need help. Set up your small-group work to allow time before and after to assist the play process.

Play influences children's thought and language significantly. It allows children to think and do with language and literacy at a higher level than when in a real situation. It prepares them for abstract ideas and thinking that further oral language comprehension. Because play requires children to conform to roles and rules, it helps them practice self-regulation in their thinking and actions. For these reasons, you need to be planful and purposeful in helping children play so as to better their talking, reading, and writing. Figure 15 describes developmental accomplishments of play that should be present by the end of kindergarten.

Standards for Work and Play

For any place to run smoothly, it is necessary to establish rules, appropriate ways of interacting, and acceptable work. Children need to know what is expected of them. It is a good idea to post a daily schedule that shows

---

Figure 15
Play Characteristics That Should Be Present by the End of Kindergarten

- Symbolic representations and symbolic actions: *Would you come with us? Let's go to Sea World.*
- Complex interwoven themes: *We're following the treasure map to the scary mountain.*
- Complex interwoven roles: *You can be the customers and I'm the cash register guy. Jared's the waiter guy. OK?*
- Extended time frame (over several days): After two days: *We're still playing hospital and the babies got so-o-o sick.*

Adapted from Bodrova & Leong (1996)

Figure 16
Play Center Board

The simplest type of management board is a pocket chart.

- Write each child's name on a card in large black letters.
- Decide how many children you want in each center. Place the names in each row of the pocket chart.
- Beside each set of names, place an icon depicting where those children are to go during play time.
- At the end of each day, move the children's names down to the next space so that their activities change for the next day.

---

the flow of the day. The schedule helps everyone to remember what comes next and also provides a written record of what has been accomplished. Discussion of the daily schedule can become part of the everyday routine and at the same time draw children's attention to print and its uses. English-language learners will find this routine extremely helpful as it will make the daily flow of activities predictable, enabling them to show that they know what is going on in the classroom.

Another helpful tool is a Play Center Board for organizing and managing children's play time (see Figure 16). You will need to teach the children how to use the board, which will require weeks of practice. But this is time well spent because it reduces interruptions while you are with small groups and it encourages children to take charge of their own learning activity. Use of the board also benefits children's print awareness because they quickly learn to recognize their own as well as their classmates' names and to connect written words with what they are doing. Some soon learn to read the words for the different play center areas.

For children to work independently at an activity they need to know the rules that apply and the consequences of not abiding by the rules. You should ask the children to help you make the rules for work and play. One way to begin is to ask the children why it is necessary to have rules. Make a list of their responses on chart paper. Ask them what would be good rules for playtime activities. List these as well. Usually children come up with negative statements, such as "No hitting." When all the children have had a chance to contribute, ask them to help you group like rules into categories: for example, No hitting, No punching, Don't throw books, Don't spit on books, Don't leave things out, and Don't yell at each other. Ask the children to help you make a label for each group and guide them toward positive statements such as Treat others kindly, Work together, Make room for others, Put things away, Use materials carefully, and Use quiet voices.

Post the rules where children can easily see them, and refer to them when introducing new activities. If you consistently refer to the rules from the beginning of the year, children will soon learn what is expected of them in work and play activities. If you find that there are English-language learners who are having difficulty with the rules, it may be that there is miscommunication about what is expected. Working directly with parents around these issues and asking parents to explain the rules to their children may help the situation.

Making the Most of Resources

Every early childhood setting contains resources in terms of time, space, people, and materials. Your careful use of these resources can maximize children's language and literacy experiences to the fullest. You need to set up your daily schedule with an emphasis on children's active learning with you and their peers in uninterrupted time blocks. Snack Time, for example, is an informal time for talking, reading, and writing, just as Nap Time is a stretch of time for hearing stories and pretending to read all by oneself. Figure 17 is an example of daily schedules in four different settings.

Adults are one of the richest resources for children because they can bring considerable knowledge, language, and print to them. One effective way to involve adults is to have them participate in topics or themes you are exploring with the children. For example, when Ben Mardell's preschoolers' studied squirrels, he invited Judy Chupasko from the Mammalian Department at Harvard University's Museum of Comparative Zoology to his class (Mardell, 1999). Judy explained the preparation of animals used in scientific study, which fascinated the children and also introduced them to the idea of anatomy—mapping the insides of things.

Another effective strategy for involving adults meaningfully is to have them join play groups. The adults can watch and learn, they can take roles and participate, or they can show children how to play a game. The adults' presence is encouraging to children and stimulates them to play for longer periods of time. When adults join in they engage children in conversation, they use new words and more complex sentences that enrich children's speaking and listening.

Materials are the stock-in-trade of a well-provisioned early learning environment. Along with everyday supplies such as writing tools, equip-

Figure 17
Sample Daily Schedules

Jacob's Day at Preschool

9:00	Jacob arrives and engages in free play
9:30–9:45	Group time
9:45–11:00	Guided learning/creative-activity time
11:00–11:50	Outdoor play
11:50–12:00	Transition to lunch
12:00–1:00	Lunch
1:00–1:10	Transition to naptime
1:10–2:30	Nap time
2:30–3:00	Free play
3:00–3:30	Snack and transition to outdoor play
3:30–4:30	Outdoor play
4:30–5:30	Guided learning/creative activity time

Lenny's Day at Family Day Care

7:00–8:00	Arrival
8:00	Breakfast
8:30	Play time (choices in play activities)
10:00	Snack
10:30	Group activity time (adult-led activities like read-alouds, storytelling, singing)
12:00	Lunch
12:45	Nap time
3:00	Snack
3:30	Group activity time
4:00	Play time
5:00	TV time
5:30	Depart

Shira's Day at Full-Day Day Care

7:30	Arrival; cozy time reading books with staff member or self-selected materials available
8:30–9:15	Breakfast
9:15–9:45	Large-group time
9:45–10:00	Transition to activity
10:00–11:40	Indoor or outdoor activity that includes small-group activities
11:40–12:00	Transition to lunch
12:00–12:45	Family-style lunch
12:45–1:00	Transition to nap
1:00–3:00	Naptime; snack as they awaken
3:30	Snack completed; indoor/outdoor child-directed play with special activities planned
4:40	Clean-up time, then songs and stories and/or quiet manipulatives as parents pick children up

Julia's Day at Half-Day Prekindergarten

7:55	Children arrive and sign in
8:00–8:50	Circle time, shared reading, and instruction
8:50–9:50	Centers
9:50–10:05	Snack time
10:05–10:35	Music, Physical Education, Art, or Computer on alternate days
10:35–10:50	Read aloud
10:50–11:05	Prepare for dismissal
11:05	Dismissal

Schedules compiled by Sandra Twardosz, University of Tennessee, Knoxville, Tennessee, USA.

ment, and charts, they include the books, toys, software, and websites that widen the world of preschoolers. Materials should be of high quality to engage preschoolers' busy minds as well as their active bodies. The Evaluation Checklist for Books, Toys, and Websites and Software in Figure 18 provides a good start for choosing high-quality materials that meet your oral language goals.

Figure 18
Evaluation Checklist for Books, Toys, and Websites and Software

Books

1. Is the book age appropriate?
   - The children can relate the story to their lives and past experiences.
   - The children can identify with characters.
   - There is directly quoted conversation.
   - The children will benefit from the attitudes and models in the story.

2. Does the book teach early literacy?
   - The book can be used to expand knowledge.
   - There is new related vocabulary.
   - The book increases or broadens understanding.
   - The book is clearly written with a vocabulary and sequence that the children can understand.
   - Repetitions of words, actions, rhymes, or story parts are used.
   - The story structure is evident with a beginning, middle, and end.
   - The story includes humorous events and silly names.

3. What are some key criteria in choosing books?
   - The text is not too long to sit through.
   - There are not too many words to read.
   - There are enough colorful or action-packed pictures or illustrations to hold the children's attention.
   - The children can participate in the story by speaking or making actions.
   - The story is not too complex, symbolic, or confusing for the children.

Toys

1. Is the toy age appropriate?
   - The toy is the correct age level for the children.
   - Special instructions are not necessary to play with the toy.
   - Children cannot harm themselves unintentionally with the toy.

2. Does the toy teach early literacy?
   - The toy can be used in relation to storytelling.
   - The toy provides opportunities to expand vocabulary.
   - The toy has writing on it that correlates with actions being done.
   - There are opportunities for children to practice new vocabulary while using the toy.
   - The toy increases or broadens understanding.

(continued)

---

3. What are some key criteria in choosing toys?
   • The children are interested in the toy.
   • The toy is reusable.
   • The toy can be integrated into current or future lessons.
   • The toy is durable.
   • There are materials included with the toy for parents/teacher to use with the toy.

Websites and Software

1. Is the website or software age appropriate?
   • The children can understand the directions to use the website or software.
   • The instructions are easy to follow or relay to the children.
   • The website or software provides separate instructions for the parent or teacher.

2. Does the website or software teach early literacy?
   • The website or software can be used by the parent or teacher in a special way.
   • The website or software offers new vocabulary.
   • The website or software increases or broadens understanding.
   • The website or software is written clearly with a vocabulary and sequence that children can understand.
   • There are repetitions of words, actions, or rhymes.
   • The website or software has humorous parts and silly names.

3. What are some key criteria in choosing a proper website or software?
   • The parent or teacher enjoys using the website or software.
   • There are no confusing parts that the teacher or parent does not understand.
   • The children are able to follow the instructions with a parent or teacher present.
   • The software or website increases in skill level and has the children's skills increase, offering more challenges.

Early childhood settings where children talk, read, and write a lot are the result of planning. When you make the effort to coordinate expectations, assessment information, activities, and resources in long- and short-term plans, you go a long way toward ensuring a high-quality learning environment for all the children in your program.

CHAPTER 4

Creating Learning Conditions for Progress in Talking, Reading, and Writing

Children grow smarter when

- they use what they already know to make sense of new information,
- they build understandings with facts and ideas, and
- they learn to check their own thinking and compare their performance to an expectation or goal.

You can use these fundamentals of learning to create conditions that give children a good start in talking, reading, and writing. Conditions are the stipulations and provisions you put into place to ensure children's progress. They include the settings, materials, experiences, and social support that create a positive climate and a strong community for learning. Rich everyday conversation, instruction, guided participation, language scaffolds, and plenty of practice are the essential ingredients of nurturing conditions. The best conditions also include your keen attention to children's **oral language comprehension, vocabulary, alphabet knowledge, phonological awareness,** and **print knowledge** development.

Everyday Conversation

We know that talking to and with children is essential. Everyday conversation is children's richest source of information about words, their meanings, and the rules of social engagement. Lacking conversation opportunities, children have trouble knowing enough words to learn from others and to keep up with their peers.

As a preschool teacher, you need to engage children in substantive conversations regularly and frequently. You need to constantly work at this in two ways.

1. *Make a conscious effort to expand the amount of child talk in a round of conversation.* We encourage at least two child turns in most rounds of conversation.

The following shows a conversation with Zach, a 3-year-old, who is on his way to the doctor for his annual checkup. The week before, Zach had accompanied his mother and his brother Matthew to the doctor. Matthew needed a throat culture, and this is on Zach's mind. Notice how Zach takes four turns in this conversation.

● ● ● ● ● ● ● ● ● ● ● ● ● ● ●

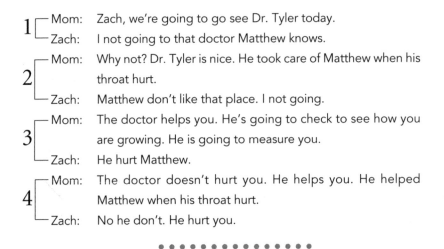

1
  Mom: Zach, we're going to go see Dr. Tyler today.
  Zach: I not going to that doctor Matthew knows.

2
  Mom: Why not? Dr. Tyler is nice. He took care of Matthew when his throat hurt.
  Zach: Matthew don't like that place. I not going.

3
  Mom: The doctor helps you. He's going to check to see how you are growing. He is going to measure you.
  Zach: He hurt Matthew.

4
  Mom: The doctor doesn't hurt you. He helps you. He helped Matthew when his throat hurt.
  Zach: No he don't. He hurt you.

● ● ● ● ● ● ● ● ● ● ● ● ● ● ●

When they got to the doctor, Zach sat on his mother's lap during the checkup with his hand over his mouth. The doctor never got to look into his mouth.

2. *Strive to stretch the conversation to add details, new words, and new language structures, such as adjectives and adverbs.* Stress the sounds of interesting, new words. Encourage children to try to say words they don't yet know. (Figure 19 shows a variety of conversation stretchers to use with children.)

Instructional Approaches

Children cannot learn the full complement of language skills for school readiness through everyday conversation alone. To master the less obvious skills of oral language and literacy, such as how to listen for the number of words in a sentence (phonological awareness) or how to spell your own name, children must be taught or tutored. If children are to properly practice and acquire more difficult skills, they need to be clearly shown what it is they need to pay attention to and how. At times, therefore, your instruction should be explicit, which is not to say it cannot be playful. Your tone of voice, demeanor, energy level, and sense of humor are means

Figure 19
Conversation Stretchers

Add Details

Teacher: What would you do if you found a dinosaur cave?
Child: I would leave it alone.
Teacher: Why would you leave it alone?
Child: 'Cause I don't want to bring it home.
Teacher: No?
Child: They would have to make a big door.
Teacher: A *gigantic* door.
Child: And a bigger house.

Explain Terms

Child: It was hot in here and that made all the water vaporate and that vaporation makes flowers droop.
Teacher: Yes, water evaporates from the soil when it's hot, and then the plant doesn't have enough. It wilts or droops.

Share Experiences

Teacher: So you went to the aquarium. When I went I was fascinated by the beautiful colors of the different small fishes.
Child: I saw a porpoise and the lady said they are NOT fish. They don't even have scales! Not everything that swims in the ocean is a fish, you know.

Wonder Aloud

Child: And I saw a ladybug beetle in my Grandma's garden. She put ladybugs in her garden to eat aphids...yucky juice-suckers.
Teacher: I wonder if aphids are beetles? They weren't mentioned in the beetle book we read. We should look that up.

you can use to tell, show, and explain to children in a playful way what they need to know and be able do. Several instructional approaches are described in chapter 5. You can use them to help children gain ground in the harder-to-learn skills of oral language comprehension, vocabulary, alphabet letter knowledge, and phonological awareness. In the following vignette, pay attention to how Hannah, the older sister, provides explicit instruction to her little sister.

• • • • • • • • • • • • • • • •

Hannah: OK. Make an *A*, Emma. Make an *A*, okay? (Hannah makes an *A* for Emma to trace. She next holds Emma's hand in hers. Together they draw an *A*.) EMMIE!!! I helped her! I helped her!

Emma: (speaking to Hannah) I want to make for you. (She works
           on the *A* some more, and then puts little marks beside
           it.)

• • • • • • • • • • • • • • • • •

Guided Participation

Through your interactions with children, you can stretch their ability to
know and use language. Simply being with children, however, is not
enough to help them learn the harder language and literacy skills necessary
for school. What makes a difference is the nature of the interaction between
you and the children in the activity. For the activity to be fruitful, you need
to guide the interaction by being sensitive and responsive to children's
motivation, attention, and competence. You need to help them focus their
attention on an activity, model or simplify the activity to maintain attention, point out the nature of their mistakes, and make adjustments to bring
about a satisfying experience for all involved. Here timing is very important: You want your feedback (gestures and words) to be contingent on or
well timed with children's efforts in order to enhance the learning power of
your time together. You can use the Guided Participation Framework (see
Figure 20) to organize your interactions with children and to reflect on
your own performance.

In the scene that follows, a teacher and child are seated together at a
table. The child is writing a greeting with crayons and markers. Notice how
the teacher uses guided participation.

• • • • • • • • • • • • • • • • •

Teacher: You can write a little. Very nice. You can write *To Mom* or
           to whomever you're going to give it (a greeting card) to.
Child: To nobody.
Teacher: To nobody. Okay. But how...okay, but how do you think
           you spell *nobody* (saying the word slowly with emphasis
           on the first syllable)?
Child: *N...O...*
Teacher: Good. And then what? *B-o-d-y.*
Teacher: Okay. You've got the *no* part. What would you? How
           would you?
Child: *B*
Teacher: Good! Good! Now?

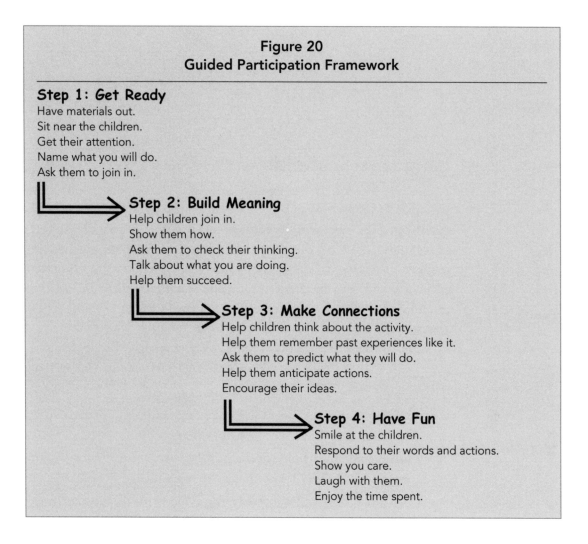

Figure 20
Guided Participation Framework

Step 1: Get Ready
Have materials out.
Sit near the children.
Get their attention.
Name what you will do.
Ask them to join in.

Step 2: Build Meaning
Help children join in.
Show them how.
Ask them to check their thinking.
Talk about what you are doing.
Help them succeed.

Step 3: Make Connections
Help children think about the activity.
Help them remember past experiences like it.
Ask them to predict what they will do.
Help them anticipate actions.
Encourage their ideas.

Step 4: Have Fun
Smile at the children.
Respond to their words and actions.
Show you care.
Laugh with them.
Enjoy the time spent.

Child:	*A?*
Teacher:	Close. It's a vowel. It has a funny sound.
Child:	*E?*
Teacher:	No, well the next letter after the *B* would be *O. NO-BO-O-O-O...D* (emphasizing the /d/ sound). What letter is this?
Child:	*D!*
Teacher:	Good. And then what? Now the last one is really hard. *NO-BOD-Y* (emphasizing the /ē/ sound of *y*). It sounds like, it sounds like...
Child:	*E!*

Teacher:	Yes, yes. It sounds like an *E*, but there's a letter way over here (points to alphabet chart) that sounds like that sometimes. Like the *E*, but it's the *Y*.
Child:	To Nobody, Love Ingrid.

• • • • • • • • • • • • • • • •

Language Scaffolds

Scaffolding is a term used to describe how adults help children learn complex tasks and skills. When children are learning to use language, adults frequently present them with mature speech. But they do so with supports or scaffolds so children can grasp the meaning. They restate sentences, repeat important words, use gestures, and respond to the children's utterances. They act as if the children can understand everything and are thus responding to what the children will do in the future but cannot yet do. This scaffolding pulls children forward to higher levels of performance.

For children to progress in their use of language, you need to provide them with a steady supply of language scaffolds in your setting (Bodrova & Leong, 1996). You should

- Label your own actions as you carry them out (e.g., "I am writing a list of the supplies we need for our field trip.").
- Label children's actions for them as they occur (e.g., "You are pouring sand into a very tall container.").
- Use explicit terms about objects (e.g., "Hand me the small hammer to pound this nail.") and about behaviors (e.g., "When you pay attention, your body is still and does not wiggle; your eyes are here and you are thinking about this book.").
- Think aloud (e.g., "Which of these objects is bigger, I wonder? How can I figure this out? Oh, I could put them side by side. If I look across, I can see which one is bigger.").
- Ask children to talk about what they are thinking (e.g., "Does what Jared told us about the road sound slushy to you?").
- Tie new words and ideas to action (e.g., "When we want to measure something to see how long it is, we put the ruler at the end of the object and read the numbers here." [teacher points]).
- Encourage children to use self-talk to learn and remember. To learn: "You can whisper to yourself while you do the puzzle to help you

think." To remember: "Let's say this three times and put it in our memory bank." (Teacher points to forehead.) "Put the caps on the paints." (Teacher puts cap on paint jar.) "Put the caps on the paints. Put the caps on the paints."

- Encourage writing (e.g., "You can make a note about what you saw the gerbil do. There's paper and markers at the writing table.").

Plenty of Practice

From science we know that there is a relationship between children's ability to use language and their growing literacy abilities (Shonkoff & Phillips, 2000; Snow, Burns, & Griffin, 1998). As they recognize words and meanings in conversations ("Where's the sheep's *tongue*?"), as they talk about words ("I don't like that word, *sneakers*. Don't say it, OK?"), and as they talk about their thinking ("I was thinking about when that bee stinged me. It hurt so-o-o-o bad!"), children are strengthening their abilities to use language to organize their ideas and to remember.

These are the same mental skills that they need to decode print and to comprehend it. They must map the sounds of language to alphabet symbols and remember printed words. They must organize the ideas presented in print and connect them to ideas already organized in their own minds.

Because these mental skills are so essential to oral language and literacy development and growth, children need many opportunities to practice using language to organize their ideas and to remember. You help children exercise these very important mental skills when you regularly use the strategies that follow.

Plan for Play

Play is most beneficial for learning when it involves pretending and creating a play story that lasts for an extended period of time. You can enrich the learning power of play when you help children plan for it (Soderman, Gregory, & O'Neill, 1999).

Here's the procedure for play planning:

1. Provide background knowledge for a new play idea by reading to children or going on a field trip.

2. Ask the children to help you change a play setting for the new play theme.

3. On chart paper, print the name of the play theme (e.g., The Kids' Café).

4. Ask children to tell you things that this play setting will need to work. Write down their ideas. Remind children to listen carefully. Someone else may have thought of their idea already. If so, children can put up a thumb so that others know they had that idea too. (You may end here for the day or continue.)

5. Ask the children to suggest where the class might get these items. Note the source next to the items on the list (e.g., *Miss Carol's house, Tanya's house, the center, a store*).

6. Have the children help you decide how to get the supplies—ask for donations, bring them in from home, etc. Make decisions about who will bring in the supplies.

7. As the supplies come in, check them off the list. This can be done at the start of play time or during group time. Have the children help you compose and mail thank-you notes to those who contributed.

8. Meanwhile, ask the children: "What roles do we need for this play idea?" List the roles with a job description for each (e.g., *Waiter: takes orders, delivers food, tells the cook what to make*).

9. With the children's help, set up the play setting during play time or tell them you will be setting it up and to look for it the next day.

10. As the play begins, move it along by asking questions, such as "How will I know the Café is open?" to motivate reading and writing or by taking a role to model the use of language and introduce new words.

Use the Language Experience Approach

The Language Experience Approach (LEA) is a longtime favorite of both adults and children. It involves child dictation of a common experience with the adult as the scribe. Language experience dictation holds a wealth of opportunity for children to use language and to see literacy in action modeled by the adult. Even better, it results in a written text that children can revisit often to remember and try reading on their own. The basic procedure is outlined in Figure 21.

Use Dialogic Reading Techniques

Dialogic reading is a conversation between an adult and children about a book. To have a substantive conversation that extends children's use of

---

Figure 21
Engaging Children in a Language Experience

Step 1: Have a Common Experience
Share a common experience with children, such as a nature walk, field trip, guest presentation, or special event.

Step 2: Take Dictation
Ask the children to help you remember the event by writing about it. Have them recall highlights and write their comments on chart paper. Read back each child's contribution, pointing to the printed words. Talk about what the words look like and how they sound. Compliment the children on their word choices.

Step 3: Read the Story
Once you have a complete story that captures the common experience (about four or five sentences), read the text to the children. Then read it again and invite the children to read along with you as you reread the piece. Finally, read it one more time. This time, pause to let individual children "read" portions of the story.

Step 4: Explore the Story
Now have some fun with the story. Engage children in discovering letters ("Let's find all the M's in this story and circle them with a red marker") or words ("Let's look for that word *geranium*. Remember we saw those beautiful red flowers on our walk."). Help them search and find specific alphabet letters and words. Help them listen for sounds in key words.

Step 5: Read the Story Again
Post the story on an easel for reading again at a later time. At each return to the story, make instructional points related to oral language comprehension, vocabulary, phonological awareness, and alphabet letters. Provide copies for children to "read" on their own and to take home.

---

language, you need to apply a set of prompts. You can remember these prompts with the word CROWD (Bowman, Donovan, & Burns, 2001).

C stands for *completion prompts*. You leave a blank at the end of a sentence for children to fill in: "Jack and Jill went up the hill to fetch a pail of _____." This prompt exercises children's sensitivity to the structure of language.

R refers to *recall prompts* that encourage children to remember what happened in the book. You say, "The little red hen wanted to make some bread. Do you remember what happened when she asked for some help?" Use this prompt to help children organize the story and remember its sequence.

O means *open-ended prompts* that focus on the pictures in books. You might say, "It's your turn to read the story. What is happening on this page?" When you encourage children to help tell the story, you provide practice in expressive fluency and attention to detail in illustrations.

W prompts include *what, where, when, and why* questions that also focus on the pictures in books. When you ask, "What's this?" you are teaching children new words. When you ask, "Why do you think the puppy is sad?" you are encouraging them to retrieve words from their own vocabulary store to express their opinions.

D stands for *distancing prompts* that guide children to make connections between the book and their experience. Reading *Brown Bear, Brown Bear, What Do You See?* you ask, "Do you have goldfish at your house? Does your goldfish have a name?" Distancing allows children to practice their conversational and storytelling skills.

Provide Sing, Say, Read, Write Pocket Charts

Songs, rhymes, and poems are an ever-fresh source of delight for young children. And in their playful way, these ways with words improve children's memory, phonological awareness, vocabulary, and creative uses of language. On occasion you should capture the joy of songs, rhymes, and poems by writing them down and displaying them in pocket charts for children to sing, say, read, and write on their own. Here's what to do over time:

1. Choose a song, chant, or poem.
2. Sing, chant, or say the selection with children. Have them repeat phrases after you to help them learn the piece.
3. Write the words on sentence strips in front of the children. Say each word as you write the phrases and sentences. Then sing, chant, or say each phrase or sentence as the children watch. Invite them to chime in. Place the strip in the pocket chart. When the entire selection is placed in the chart, sing, chant, or say it through in its entirety while pointing to the words.
4. Have the children close their eyes and mix up the sentence strips. After they open their eyes have them help you put the strips back in order. Be prepared for a lot of language!

Use a Wall Calendar for Daily News

A wall calendar is a good way to enrich your setting with print and to provide opportunities for children to talk, read, and write on topics of special interest to them. It also presents a refreshing supplement to the traditional calendar approach by including Daily News and increasing the number of children who can participate in calendar activities. Here's how:

1. Select a wall space for the calendar. You will need enough space to display five 8½-by-11-inch (22-by-28 cm.) sheets of manila paper —one for each day of the week.

2. During Calendar Time, have an 8½-by-11-inch sheet of paper ready on a nearby easel.

3. Following your calendar routine, work with the children to record the following information on the manila paper: day of the week, date, weather, and one newsworthy item (e.g., *We are going to the bakery today.*). Write the text in large print.

4. Ask for a volunteer or two who will make a drawing for the calendar page at the art table. Talk about what the drawing might be and what colors to use. Be sure to make a note of who is illustrating the page for the day.

5. Collect the calendar page at the end of the day. Consider any other additions, such as photos or three-dimensional items that might increase interest and add visual detail. Attach the page to the wall or a wire in sequence as the days of the week pass.

6. Each day, review the Calendar Wall with the children. Help them remember past events and recall details for each day. Have them practice remembering the names of the days of the week and counting.

7. Repeat steps 1–6 for each week of the month. If possible, display each week, moving each passing week further up the wall to create a giant calendar of the month. Put a pointer by the calendar so that children can locate specific days and view, read, and remember events that have passed.

8. When the month has passed, assemble the pages into a book. Make a cover (e.g., *The Merry Month of May*). Put it in the library center for children to look at and read on their own.

Use Nursery Rhymes

Without a doubt, young children need to hear, say, and learn nursery rhymes. Not only do children love the lilt and lyric of these jingles, they also benefit immensely from them in terms of their developing phonological awareness—the ability to hear the sound structure of words. Children are drawn to the "tumble-down" of "Humpty Dumpty," the action of "Cobbler, Cobbler," and the awful plight of "Little Miss Muffet." There should be no day without nursery rhymes in your preschool classroom. The following webites offer fresh ideas and resources for using nursery rhymes regularly in your program:

- www.mamalisa.com—Houses traditional Mother Goose nursery rhymes as well as nursery rhymes and songs from all nations.
- www.hendersonville-pd.org/hpdnursery.html—Features audio for each nursery rhyme.
- www.preschoolrainbow.org/preschool-rhymes.htm—Groups fingerplays, action poems, nursery rhymes, and songs according to early childhood education themes.

Use Signature and Name Games

One of the first words that children learn to read is their own first name. Much treasure can be gained in language and literacy from this small discovery. Using signature and name games, you can begin to teach children to recognize and name familiar alphabet letters in their own names, to learn more letters in other children's names, and to listen for sounds associated with syllables and letters in names. Try the following games.

Add Signatures to Important Documents.
Establish this practice early and provide many opportunities for children to sign their names. For example, establish a sign-in procedure for your classroom. Have an attendance sheet for each day—one that is stamped with the date but otherwise blank. Place it and a pencil in the same place each day, and teach children to sign in when they arrive. These attendance sheets will make interesting records of the consistencies and changes over time in the way children print their name. Later in the year, you might have children add one sentence to their name when they sign in, telling something about how they are feeling that day or an item of personal "news."

Compose some of your notes to families with the help of your class. You can transcribe the children's suggestions onto note paper to be photocopied. Each child can sign his or her own copy to take home (using a name tag as a model, if necessary). Each note that goes home can come from you and from the children. Show children where you have signed your name and the spaces where they should print theirs.

Develop group charts such as the classroom rules and have everyone sign them. Explain that each signature means that that child has agreed to do his or her best to follow the rules.

Incorporate forms appropriate to each dramatic-play center for children to sign. For example, include forms for prescriptions at the Doctor's Office.

Playing Name Games. A variety of short games can be devised for use with small groups, pairs, or individuals. Here are some examples of short name games:

Follow My Directions if Your Name Has This Letter in It. Say the name of a letter and write it on the chalkboard and ask students to follow your directions only if their name starts with the letter you write. For example, say and write an uppercase letter and then say, "Clap two times if your name starts with this letter." Alternate this with lowercase letters, writing the letter and saying its name followed by a direction like "Put one hand under your chin if your name ends with this letter." Or use at dismissal time, "Those whose name begins like this may get ready for home." Or, "If you have the letter *e* anywhere in your name, you may get ready for snack."

Name Bingo. Give each child a card with his or her name on it (initially just the first name, later include middle and last names) and a set of plastic chips. Tell the children, "I will call out the name of a letter and write it on the board. If your name has that letter in it, cover it with a plastic chip. When all the letters in your name are covered, hold up your hand and say *Bingo.*" At the end of each round, have children switch name cards so that they learn the letters in other children's names as well.

Name Scramble. Give each child a card with his or her name printed on it and have the children cut their name cards into smaller cards, each one with a letter of their name on it. Ask children to scramble the letters on a table and then put them back in order to spell their name. (Demonstrate this first.) Have children trade cards and see if they can unscramble a different name. Refer them to the attendance chart, or another chart with class names on it, if they need help. They could also ask the person whose name they have for one clue to get them started.

Name Riddles. Make up riddles using children's names. For example, "I am thinking about a boy who has two *o*'s in his name." Encourage the children to make up name riddles as well.

What About English-Language Learners?

But what about working with English-language learners? Will you need to change the way you think about creating learning conditions for talking, reading, and writing for these students? The answer is, Not at all. Except, perhaps at first, you will need to do more of the talking. But don't be discouraged that an English-language-learning child does not respond right away to your attempts at conversation. Remember that there is likely to be a nonverbal period for English-language learners when they will be trying to make sense of the new language that is being used in the classroom. During that time they will be getting used to the new sounds of the language and will be beginning to try to understand what different words mean. They will not start using their new language until they feel comfortable that they have something to say and they know the right way to say it. And even after they begin to use their new language, there will be a lot that they won't know how to say. By carefully setting up everyday conversations, guided participation, and language scaffolds, you will be helping the English-language learners as well as the other children in your classroom. So, even if the English-language learners aren't using their new language yet, they are developing important information. And when they do start to use their new language all of these techniques will help them to learn more quickly.

Children thrive in conditions that nurture their language discoveries, their different uses of language, and their first attempts to read and write. You create these conditions when you engage children in meaningful conversations, assist them in meeting new learning challenges, and offer them opportunities for practice that are engaging and worthwhile. Under these conditions, the children in your program are off to a good start as accomplished speakers, listeners, readers, and writers.

CHAPTER 5

Using Instructional Approaches to Teach Oral Language and Early Literacy

An instructional approach is a learning context that you can use to purposefully teach children about language and how to use it effectively. In the early childhood setting, there are a few time-honored instructional approaches that work very well. Used routinely, they provide dependable educational frameworks that encourage children to join in, focus their attention, and use language to organize their thinking. In the case of instructional approaches, less is more. When children are accustomed to a few routines, much that is new can be incorporated into them. Learning new words, new sounds, and new concepts is easier when it occurs in a familiar learning context, such as storybook reading or singing a song.

Six Instructional Approaches

In this chapter you will learn about six instructional approaches that create powerful learning contexts in which children can explore, learn, and use language in ways that advance their talking, reading, and writing. They are

- singing and rhyming
- storytelling
- shared reading
- shared writing
- show and tell
- guided play

Each approach is described briefly, followed by an explanation of what the approach has to offer as an oral language and early literacy builder, especially in developing the skills of **oral language comprehension**, **vocabulary**, **alphabet knowledge**, **phonological awareness**, and **print knowledge**. How each approach connects to early learning **standards** in **language** and **literacy**, and thus supports school readiness, is also shown. A protocol, or procedure, that typifies each instructional approach is given, and key organizational features are highlighted and illustrated in a sample lesson, each with a before, during, and after phase.

Singing and Rhyming

For centuries children have found satisfaction in singing simple songs and repeating short rhymes. It is the pleasure of playing with sound that makes it fun to sing songs and say rhymes. Exactly what the words mean is unimportant. **Word play** is the reason why preschool teachers should sing songs and say rhymes often with children. The teaching objectives are to help children listen on purpose for sounds in language and to pronounce new sounds and words. Along with children's obvious delight in singing and rhyming, they practice focusing their attention on similarities and differences in combinations of sounds, which sharpens their phonological awareness. They also are exposed to difficult new words that challenge and exercise their speaking abilities. Perhaps not surprising, singing songs and saying rhymes are activities that help English-language learners use their new language orally for the first time. The elements of playing with sounds, group recitation, and movement all seem to make it easier for English-language learners to participate and "go public," sometimes as loudly as possible.

It is especially noteworthy that the predictable patterns found in many songs, rhymes, chants, and fingerplays help children develop sensitivity to ending sounds that are alike (e.g., *Ding dong, bell / Pussy's in the well / Who put her in? / Little Tommy Green / Who pulled her out? / Big Johnny Stout*). Hearing similar ending sounds is an early step in developing a concept of word in print. Figure 22 provides some examples of language play.

Figure 22
Play With Sounds and Words

- Hearing rhyming words: *Jack be nimble, / Jack be quick; / Jack jump over the candlestick.*
- Hearing alliteration: *Little Robin Redbreast / Sat upon a rail; / Niddle, naddle went his head / Wiggle, waggle went his tail.*
- Saying difficult words: *Little Miss Muffet / Sat on a tuffet, / Eating her curds and whey....*
- Being clever with language: *Hicka, Vicka, Sola Nick / Chicka, Bicka, Boo / Voolee, Voolee Voolee, Voolee, I Pick You* (4-year old Claudia's chant for choosing who will be first).

Connection to Early Learning Standards. Most sets of early learning standards include a phonological awareness standard. The Head Start Outcomes Framework (see Figure 23) includes this standard supported by five indicators.

The instructional approach of singing and rhyming richly addresses this standard because it offers many opportunities for developing children's language and phonological awareness. Actively engaged in songs, chants, rhymes, and fingerplays, children learn to attend to sounds in language and to pronounce new words. When you help children to differentiate between sounds that are the same and different, to recognize when words share sounds, and to snap and clap along, you are showing them how to listen on purpose for specific rhyming sounds, for individual words in sentences, for syllables in a word, and for beginning sounds. This instruction prepares the way for children's phonemic awareness—the critical ability to hear and manipulate the sound structure of individual words.

Organizing for a Singing or Rhyming Session. To teach singing and rhyming in a way that maximizes learning, follow this basic protocol.

Begin with the joy of singing and rhyming:

1. Introduce a new song or rhyme with enthusiasm and gusto.

2. Ask children to guess what the song or poem might be about by using a puppet, prop, or picture to provide clues.

3. Sing or play a recording of the song a few times, inviting children to sing it with you. Similarly, say the new poem a few times and then ask children join in saying it with you.

4. Add movement by having the children snap, clap, or sway with the rhythm of the song or poem.

Then make the words of the song or poem both visible and physical:

5. Encourage children to guess the next words in a phrase, using pictures or gestures as clues.

6. Print the song or poem on a chart, adding rebus pictures for some of the key words.

7. Add physical movement to enhance the feel of the words.

Sample Singing Lesson: "Old MacDonald Had a Farm"

Objectives

- Practice producing environmental sounds and associating them with the appropriate source.
- Play with and manipulate phonemes within the song (e.g., replace the first phoneme of an animal's sound with the initial letter of its name, as in *A cow says, "Coo-coo-coo, cei, cei, o"; A duck says, "Dack, dack, dack with a dei, dei, o."*).
- Build vocabulary skills by introducing other animals (silly as well as logical) on the farm (e.g., giraffe).
- Foster enjoyment of singing together.

Before: Introduce the children to farmyard puppets and discuss the sounds they make. Ask for suggestions of animals that don't generally live on a farm—Where do these animals live? What sounds do they make? Categorize the suggested animals into wild, domestic, and farm animals.

During: Have the children sing along. Offer other suggestions of animals on the farm, then invite the children to do so. Record their verses on chart paper. Read and sing the new verses together. Help the children replace the initial phoneme of each animal sound with that of the animal's name (as indicated above).

After: Provide mural paper for children to paste cutouts and draw pictures (real and silly) of the animals on Old MacDonald's Farm. Provide puppets for the children to use during activity time as they sing and play with the sounds.

Singing songs and saying rhymes offer many opportunities for children to use language in a fun way. Through songs and rhymes children are naturally exposed to new words, repetitive text, sounds, memorable phrases, and other language patterns that are critical for later reading and writing.

Storytelling

Storytelling is an ancient form of instruction used by all cultures to teach young children about the world. It is also one of the earliest expressions of the language arts to appear in children. Every child has a story to tell and seeks an audience (even sleepy dogs and mute dolls) who will listen with rapt attention. Kirk, age 4, is a typical preschool storyteller.

● ● ● ● ● ● ● ● ● ● ● ● ● ● ● ●

Once there was a doggy and a little boy. The doggy was pretty silly. He ran away from the little boy and went father and farther away. The little boy caught the doggy with his hands. He put the doggy down. The doggy ran away again. He came near a railroad track. He stepped on it and the train ran over him. But he was still alive. This was a big white bulldog and he wanted to go back to his home. When the little boy came back home he found the doggy. He was happy. His doggy was still alive. (Daniels & Zemelman, 1985, p. 222)

● ● ● ● ● ● ● ● ● ● ● ● ● ● ● ●

Among the different instructional approaches commonly used in early childhood settings, storytelling is one of the most valuable for developing children's oral language comprehension. In order to understand a story, children must be active listeners. They must make predictions, use context clues to figure out new words, and rely on their memory as the storyteller "spins" the tale. In becoming storytellers themselves, children must use their expressive vocabulary, narrative skills, and sense of audience to organize and tell a good story. Storytelling expands language experience for both tellers and listeners, providing opportunities to learn language and to learn through language.

Consider bringing storytellers from different cultures into the classroom. If these storytellers can tell tales in the home languages of the English-language learners, they will provide those children with a sense of pride in their home languages and will provide the English-speaking children with the understanding that storytelling is a part of many cultural traditions.

Connection to Early Learning Standards. The early learning standard for listening and speaking includes the expectation that children will show the ability to listen to oral stories and tell simple personal stories consisting of a sequence of events.

Active listening involves the skills of focusing attention on the speaker, recognizing word meanings, using prior experience, and exercising self-regulation to maintain effort. Adult storytelling is one of the primary means for teaching children the active listening skills necessary for narrative competence. Under your guidance, children also learn to tell their own stories. This experience provides them with opportunities to practice orally presenting ideas, to use **decontextualized** language, and to organize their thinking in story form. Telling stories allows children to show their narrative abilities and helps prepare them for learning how to read and write.

Organizing for a Teacher Storytelling Session. Good storytelling takes planning, preparation, and thoughtful story selection. The following protocol will help you plan your storytelling session.

First, select a story that you like and is appropriate to share with children. Guidelines for your decision making are listed in Figure 24.

Once you've selected your story, thoroughly familiarize yourself with it by reading or going over it until you know it, although it is not necessary to memorize it. Make sure you can remember all the relevant details and significant events in the order in which they occur. Consider creating a cue card for yourself. Next, practice your story until it is second nature to you. The story should be so well known that you can recast and reshape it

---

Figure 24
Guidelines for Selecting Tales for Storytelling

- The story is age-level appropriate with easily understood words.
- The plot has action and creates a stage for what is to come.
- The story uses repetition, rhyme, or silly words.
- The values and models presented are appropriate for today's children.
- The characters are memorable.
- Taste, smell, sight, sound, and tactile descriptions create richness and depth.
- The story line is strong, clear, and logical.
- The storyteller likes the story and is eager to share it.

From Breneman & Breneman (1983)

in response to your young listeners' needs and reactions. Additionally, you should decide whether you will use props (e.g., flannelboard figures, objects, pictures presented or sketched as you talk) and plan how and where these will be presented in the story. Consider building in repetitive phrases so children can join in ("Then I'll huff, and I'll puff, and I'll blow your house down"). Finally, rehearse the story a bit so you feel confident in your ability to share it with the children. Vary your tone, speed, volume, and pitch to make it more interesting.

Preparing Children for a Storytelling Session. You prepare children for their role as storytellers in three ways. As an adult role model, you inspire children to tell stories and also provide them with ideas about how to do it. They can use the organizational strategies you show them to fashion their own entertaining tales. Going further, regularly hold one-to-one conferences with children in the library center to assist them in creating wonderful stories of their own. Provide "editorial assistance" by suggesting props and asking leading questions about setting, character, and plot. Shortly after the preparatory conference, invite the child to the storyteller's chair and gather the other children around. As the child's story is told, provide assistance only if necessary, allowing the young storyteller to carry the responsibility for relating the tale and connecting with the audience. When done regularly and in a sensitive, supportive manner, storytelling builds children's sense of story and lifts their narrative abilities to new levels.

Sample Storytelling Lesson: "The Gingerbread Man"

    Objectives

- Gain exposure to new words found in stories.
- Listen for cues in a story and chime in appropriately.
- Build awareness of basic story structure (beginning, middle, end) through listening to stories.
- Experience clear and understandable speech.

Before: Introduce the folk tale to the class. Tell the children they will be part of the story by joining in. Teach them the part, "Run, run, as fast as you can, you can't catch me—I'm the Gingerbread Man!" Explain to the children that they should say their part when they hear you say, "The Gingerbread Man called after them...." Practice this several times.

During: Wear an apron to tell the story and have some props, such as a gingerbread cookie cutter, a rolling pin, or a spatula, to add a visual component. Children will be joining in during the repetitive parts of the story.

After: Retell this cumulative tale with a flannelboard and felt characters. As you retell the story, have children repeat the sequence to show the story's progression. During activity time, allow the children to recreate the scene and retell the story on the flannelboard.

An alert, active listener focuses attention on the speaker; responds appropriately with silence, laughter, and body language; and should be able to answer simple questions related to the story. Frequent use of storytelling as an instructional approach will build these essential listening skills.

Shared Reading

Shared reading mimics the time-honored bedtime story routine in which adult and child share the warm intimacy of reading together. In the early childhood setting, a Big Book or other enlarged text is used to share a story with the whole class or a small group of children. The Big Book allows all the children to participate actively in the reading of the story. If there are English-language learners in the class, keep in mind that a shorter reading session or one that is tailored specifically for them may work best.

After repeated readings, individual children can learn to read familiar books on their own. As a result of instruction that occurs in shared reading, children gain knowledge about books and print. They learn basic skills of book handling and make progress in following print (tracking it) as the source of the message (the ideas).

Connection to Early Learning Standards.   Shared reading is an instructional approach with tremendous educational potential for helping children meet oral language and early literacy expectations. While reading to and with children, you can easily point out key features of books (e.g., how to hold books and turn pages) and print (e.g., where the print is and how to follow it with your finger). You can model comprehension strategies by showing children how to make predictions using pictures and past experience as clues, how to check out guesses with the printed words and the story as it unfolds, and how to make connections between the story and prior experience in order to expand knowledge. You can teach vocabulary by explaining new words and discussing them with children, helping them to say new words and connecting them to what they already know.

Organizing Features of a Shared Reading Session.

Like all instruction, shared reading must be well planned if children are to receive the most benefit from the interactive experience. Keep in mind the following protocol when organizing your lessons. First, consider whether or not the book is suitable for shared reading. Texts with cumulative, repetitive, or patterned texts are best because they allow children to participate in the experience by repeating patterned lines and predicting story development.

Next, organize the lesson into three parts: *before*, *during*, and *after* shared reading. *Before* reading activities should arouse children's interest and curiosity in the book. This could include sharing of title and author, previewing and discussing the book, or experiencing an activity that is connected to the book.

During reading is the time when you use prompts, questions, and brief discussions to keep children actively engaged with the reading and invite their participation. You need to ask children questions such as "What do you think this book will be about? What makes you think that? What do you think will happen next? Why? What word do you think comes next? What other word might we use that means the same thing?" You should also stop and briefly explain new words you want the children to learn, for example, "A *ukulele* is a kind of guitar."

Immediately after reading you should proceed with two purposes in mind: (1) You want to engage the children in a discussion about the story in order to strengthen their oral language comprehension, and (2) you want to teach new words to children.

The vocabulary protocol requires you to select two or three new words to directly teach after the shared reading of a story. Select words that are (1) important and useful for children to know, (2) instructionally powerful for making connections to other words and ideas, and (3) concept building in that they expand children's understanding of the word's meaning. Consider this instructional sequence:

1. Remind children of how the word was used in the story.
2. Ask them to repeat the word so that they create a phonological or sound impression of the word in their minds.
3. Explain the meaning of the word in child-friendly language.
4. Provide examples in contexts different from the story.
5. Ask children to provide their own examples with your support.

6. Ask them to say the word again to establish their phonological awareness of it.

7. Repeat the above steps for each target word.

8. End by using all the target words together.

Later in the day and over the next few days you should make many return visits to the book in order to complete projects or activities, such as story dramas, writing activities, and play center activities (e.g., picture sorts).

Sample Shared Reading Lesson: *The Little Red Hen*

Objectives

- Build vocabulary by exposing children to new words about how bread is made.

- Listen for and establish a sequence of events in a story.

- Develop phonological awareness skills by listening to and saying words.

Before: Show children the cover of the book, read the title to them, and then invite discussion of the illustration. Ask, "What do you think this story will be about?" and "What does this cover remind you of?" Encourage predictions.

During: Read the story to the children and allow them to chime in once they pick up on the repetitive pattern of the text: "'Not I,' said the cat." *Stop* along the way and encourage predictions such as, "What do you think the dog is going to tell the little red hen when she asks for help?" or "Look at the picture. What do you think a *sickle* is?"

After: Engage the children in a discussion about the story. Encourage them to describe the characters to you and retell the story in sequence. Next, teach new words, for example, "In our story, the little red hen threshed the wheat so she could make bread. Do you remember what she did when she threshed the wheat?"

"Say the word with me: *threshed.* To thresh something means to get the grain (the seeds) out of their dry shells or their husks by hitting them. In the late summer, farmers thresh the wheat that they grow on their farms. They use big machines, called combines, to thresh the wheat."

"What else do you think farmers thresh on their farms? I am thinking of something horses like to eat. (Farmers thresh oats.) I am thinking of some seeds that birds like to eat. (Farmers thresh sunflower seeds.)"

"Say the word *thresh* with me again: thresh."

Repeat the above steps for each target word.

End by using all the target words together. Start by saying, "We talked about two new words: *thresh* and *husks*." Then, point out how they are related. "*Thresh* and *husks* are words we use to talk about harvesting wheat to make bread." Use a single context to connect them: "The Little Red Hen cut the wheat and threshed it to get the grain out of the stiff husks." Or use them in the same sentence format: "Farmers thresh wheat with big machines. Farmers get the wheat seeds from their husks."

Shared reading is an instructional approach that lends itself to many teachable moments. While teachers should be planful and purposeful, the format of shared reading allows for rich, spontaneous conversation to occur naturally around a story shared by all. Shared reading books that are new one week quickly become old favorites, requested time and again.

Shared Writing

The Russian theorist Lev Vygotsky proposed that drawing and writing are the forerunners of reading. When children draw or make scribble marks on paper, they are using symbols to express their ideas and thoughts. They are trying to communicate with you in another kind of language.

You can capitalize on children's early drawing and writing intentions by engaging them in shared writing activities that help them create messages they would be unable to do alone. Under your guidance, they can learn much about written language together. Children can learn

- how to express themselves in their own words and to see what their words look like in print;
- how to compose different kinds of messages, such as letters, invitations, stories, and the like;
- how to listen for and record sounds of words they know and new words; and
- how to form upper- and lowercase letters, and what punctuation marks are.

Shared writing enables teachers to deliberately build children's vocabulary. With frequent practice, children gain a bank of words that they can use independently to write personal messages and stories. Shared writing activities are appropriate for all children, including English-language learners. But, as with other aspects of the process of gaining competence in English, it may take longer for English-language learners to move from drawing, to being able to explain their drawings, to being able to write.

Connections to Early Learning Standards. The beginning of writing as a means of **communication** is an early literacy expectation. It is expected that by age 4 children will know how to print their own name independently and other words with assistance. They should make attempts to spell words. They also should show signs of using the writing process as a means of communication by generating ideas for drawing and writing, dictating stories, playing at writing and reading, and willingly sharing their products with others.

Shared writing is fertile ground for modeling the writing process with young children. Under your tutelage, children learn early writing strategies for generating ideas and choosing a topic (prewriting), recording words with your assistance (drafting), and displaying their work for all to read (publishing).

Organizing for a Shared Writing Session. Follow this basic protocol when leading a shared writing session with a group of children. Because shared writing is a whole-group activity, you need to gather the children around so they can easily see and approach the easel with chart paper for recording the message. After talking about what the message or story will be about, you should begin by acting as the scribe. As you go, invite children to participate by offering ideas and sharing in the writing "work."

Think aloud, asking for the children's opinions to draw them into the writing: "What would be the best word to say how we feel? I wonder what letter that word starts with. Is it *c* or *k*? Oops! I put too many *t*'s in that word. Whatever was I thinking? Am I spelling your name right, Alikah? I bet I know what you're thinking, Rodney, so you'd better tell us before I spill the beans."

Write slowly, commenting on content and mechanics. Depending on their skill and experience, ask children to help by writing a letter, showing spacing for a word, writing a word, or adding punctuation. Build their understanding as the session unfolds by pointing out how speech is transformed into written language and stating important conventions and rules. When you are done composing, read the message several times and invite the children to join in. Leave the message on the easel or post it for rereading several more times before moving on to a new composition.

Sample Shared Writing Lesson: Writing an Invitation

Objectives

• Help children express ideas through drawing and writing.

• Demonstrate how to use writing as a process of communication.

• Develop concepts about print through modeling and practice.

• Develop awareness of beginning sounds in words.

Before: Tell the children that today we are going to write an invitation to Mr. T.'s class to come and see the beautiful butterflies that emerged from their cocoons this morning. Talk about what the invitation should say: "Have you ever gotten an invitation to a friend's birthday party? What did it say? What should we write in our invitation? How should we go about it? Who has an idea?"

During: Act as the scribe. Ask the children to join in by coming to the easel and using their hand as a space holder, or filling in letters they know: "Brian, your name starts like *b/b/butterfly*. Could you come up and write a *B* for *Brian* and *butterfly*?"

Think aloud as you write, and have children suggest beginning letters as you sound out words. Allow children to draw pictures in place of some words.

After: Read the message several times. Have the children sign the message, and then discuss and decide on how you will deliver the letter to the other class.

Shared writing and drawing provide many opportunities for modeling, thinking aloud, and explicit instruction. Take full advantage of this context to present writing strategies, concepts of print, alphabet knowledge, and phonological awareness. At the same time, you are encouraging children to use language to express their ideas and feelings.

Show and Tell

Show and tell is a well-known routine that has traditionally focused on children describing familiar (and loved) objects to the group. But this familiar routine also serves as an excellent opportunity for teaching children oral language comprehension skills and new vocabulary. Early in your program year, show and tell sessions should be *guided* in order to make the communication skills to be learned explicit. Model how to present simple "news" items, emphasizing the *who, what, when, where,* and *why* of the news.

Demonstrate how to *show* an item by pointing out the most important features in a clear manner for the audience. Children should name the item and describe what it is, how it works, what it is used for, and why it was shown. Show the audience how to comment and question the speaker. As children assume more responsibility for the show and tell routine, advance their speaking and listening abilities by introducing different models of language (e.g., discussion, explanations, questioning), specialized vocabulary (e.g., theme-related words), and social interaction courtesies that develop social awareness.

Connection to the Early Learning Standards. Effective use of the language of social interaction (speaking and listening skills) is a pillar of early childhood education and a prominent oral language standard. Children need many opportunities to learn how to communicate effectively and appropriately in a variety of situations. They need specific language comprehension skills to develop social awareness. Nearly as old as early childhood education itself, show and tell is a most beneficial instructional approach for meeting this critical expectation. When well planned and well structured, it enables children to express their ideas, ask and answer questions, exchange experiences, and show consideration and respect for others. It exposes children to new words in a variety of language structures, such as discussion, problem solving, investigating, and conversations, and encourages their use of increasingly complex and varied sentences and vocabulary.

Organizing for a Show and Tell Session. For this, there are a few basic *do's* and *don'ts*. Do encourage, but don't force, children to speak. This is especially true for English-language learners. It will probably be quite some time before they feel comfortable in this situation and able to follow the format and language requirements of the activity. Use the time to teach children how to speak clearly, how to listen attentively, how to ask and answer questions, how to make judgments, and how to share new thoughts.

Do invite children to present items from home, but don't limit the children to this source only. Include sculptures, constructions, books they have written or read, or special drawings that are the results of their ongoing work and play.

Do arrange for the presenter to be clearly visible to the group. Set the expectation that the listeners must listen on purpose and be prepared to ask probing questions. But also limit the time for the presentation so that eager-to-learn children do not lose interest.

Do vary the routine now and then, but don't change it too much, because it has withstood the test of time as a beneficial learning opportunity for children. Try

- having the children swap (if possible) and discuss their items;
- bringing in a surprise item to share with the children;
- asking children to dictate a caption for their item and putting it on display; or
- placing objects in a bag and encouraging children to guess, based on clues offered by the presenter.

Sample Show and Tell Lesson

Objectives

- Speak clearly and understandably to express ideas and to answer questions.
- Listen attentively and be prepared to ask questions or comment.

Before: At the beginning of the program year, Ms. M. involves the children in an introductory theme called "Celebrating Me and My Family." She reads aloud theme-related books, such as *Lots of Moms* (Rotner & Kelly, 1996) and *Lots of Dads* (Rotner & Kelly, 1997) and *Families Share* (Williams, 2002). To become better acquainted with one another, the children discuss their own homes, the people who live there, and the things they do together. Ms. M. makes a chart listing their ideas. In a note home, parents are asked to send in one or two photos of the child with his or her family or a family member. Ms. M. brings in photos of her family and shares them with the children during group time, identifying each person. She models how to talk about *who* is in the photograph, *where* they are, and *what* they are doing together.

During: Each child gets a turn to describe his or her photograph from home to fellow playmates. With some prompting by Ms. M.—"Who is in the picture?" "What are you doing together?" "Where are you?" (at home, at a park, a picnic, or a party)—each child relates the event captured in the photograph. The other children are encouraged to ask the speaker questions, too: "Where did you get that little dog?" "How come you named him *Moose*?" Usually this requires some modeling by Ms. M. until the children come to understand the difference between a statement about their own experiences and a question about the topic.

After: Ms. M. creates a lovely photograph display that celebrates each child's family. For the display, she makes a label that tells the "Who," "Where," and "What" of each family photo. Children like to linger at the photo display, talking about their own and others' families.

Show and tell, as a basic instructional routine, is an excellent approach for building oral language. Like all the other routines, you need to be planful and purposeful as you lead this activity. It is not enough to simply allow the children to show their objects and vaguely talk about them. You must strive to advance the children's language by following an established protocol to gain the many benefits of this well-known routine as an oral language builder.

Guided Play

It is often said that young children learn best through play, and indeed they probably do. Play is an enjoyable activity in which children can exercise and stretch what they know and can do. For this reason it is referred to as a "leading" activity in early childhood because it heads children's physical, emotional, social, and cognitive development in new directions. Children really do grow stronger and smarter by playing. So it does no good to shortchange playtime in your early childhood setting. But in that same vein, while children should be in charge of their play most of the time (otherwise it is not play in their minds), you should be guiding play toward more mature uses and forms some of the time. You should plan for and use guided play to further children's language and early literacy abilities.

Guided play is play that is structured to directly teach academic skills and concepts. You might think of it as a blend of play and academic "work." It includes some of the characteristics of play (e.g., flexibility and pretending), but it is also structured by you and has a preset learning objective or objectives. It is intended to supplement the regular child-centered play experiences that children have in your setting and on the playground. As such, it does not replace "real" play. Rather it offers a middle ground for teaching and learning between free play and direct instruction and thus taps the advantages of both.

Connection to Early Learning Standards.   Both oral language and early literacy standards rest on the fundamental expectation that children should know and be able to think with symbols—both spoken and written. This requires the ability to separate thought from actions and objects in the immediate environment. For young children, this is a difficult distinction to make, because what is "here and now" has a strong pull on what they think and do. Pretend play, in particular, helps children to develop the ability to separate from the here and now ("Let's pretend we're at the beach, OK?"), to let one thing stand for another ("This block is a boat"), and to assume roles ("I'll be the mom; you be the dad").

For pretend play to occur, children must plan. They must regulate their behaviors to keep the play going. They must communicate, using meaningful gestures and language. In their effort to play for the fun of it, children must work hard mentally. And as they do, they exercise their symbolic thinking—at the same time pulling it forward to higher levels and new uses such as reading and writing. Guided play is an appropriate way to ensure ample time and assistance for developing and strengthening the symbolic thinking abilities that children need in order to make progress in oral language and early literacy.

Organizing for Guided Play.

You should plan for guided play that is logically sequenced and connected with other learning experiences. The before, during, after structure used in the preceding instructional approaches helps you accomplish this goal.

Before engaging the children in a guided play session, determine the oral language and/or early literacy objectives among the primary skill areas (oral language comprehension, vocabulary, alphabet letter knowledge, phonological awareness, and print knowledge) that you will teach. Consider potential play topics linked to your current topic or theme and invite the children to help you plan the play setting and activity. (See chapter 3 for information about how to plan for play.) Find out what children already know about the topic and include this in the development of the play setting. As needed, provide background information for enjoyable play by taking a field trip, viewing and listening to topic experts, and reading books related to the topic.

During the full swing of the play activity, observe the progress of play. Step in periodically to scaffold the play toward the desired objectives (but do not force this). You can model higher levels of play by introducing new words, new roles, and new routines that build children's knowledge of the topic or theme. Compliment the children on their growing ability to engage in play about the topic and to join in the fun with others.

After a play session or two and when children are more experienced with the theme or topic, arrange to work with small groups. Your purpose is to more explicitly connect the play experience(s) to the learning objectives. Begin by helping the children to recall their play experience—the roles they played, what they did, new words they used. Then provide instruction related to your objectives. For example, you might role-play conversations to practice pronouncing and using topic-related words or play a matching game with pictures, environmental print, or props used in the play. Allow sufficient time for each child to practice the skills related to your learning objectives.

Sample of a Guided Play Lesson: Playing Gas Station and Garage
(Adapted from Roskos, Christie, & Richgels, 2003)

> **Objectives**
>
> • Use new topic-related vocabulary words in play.
>
> • Develop children's phonological awareness skills by having them listen for the beginning sound of words.
>
> • Practice saying and using new words outside the play setting.

With the help of the children, Ms. G. creates a Gas Station/Garage dramatic-play center as part of an ongoing unit on transportation. This is how the lesson unfolds over a period of several weeks.

Before: Ms. G. provides background knowledge by reading *Sylvia's Garage* (Lee, 2002), an informational book about a mechanic. She discusses new words, such as *mechanic, engine, dipstick,* and *oil.* After reading and talking about the children's experiences with garages, she invites the children to help her plan and set up a gas station/garage dramatic-play center. She asks the children about the roles they can play (e.g., gas station attendant, mechanic, customer) and records their ideas on a piece of chart paper. She then asks the children to brainstorm some props that they could use in their center (e.g., signs, cardboard gas pump, oil can, tire pressure gauge) and jots these on another piece of chart paper. The children then decide which props they will make in class and which will be brought from home, and the teacher or a child places an *M* after each item that will be made in class and an *H* after each item that will be brought from home.

During the next several days, Ms. G. helps the children construct some of the props, such as a sign for the gas station ("*Gas* starts with a *g*. Gary, your name also starts with a *g*. Can you show us how to write a *g*?).

The list of props to be brought from home is included in the classroom newsletter and sent home to families.

During: Ms. G. first observes the children at play to learn about their current play interests and activities. Then she provides scaffolding that extends and enriches children's play and at the same time guides them to use the new topic words frequently. Ms. G. notices, for example, that the young mechanics are not using related vocabulary such as *oil, gas, tire,* and *repair,* nor are they writing service orders or bills for the customers, so she takes on a role as an assistant mechanic and models how to use the words and write out a bill for fixing a customer's car. She monitors her involvement to ensure close alignment with children's ongoing activity.

After: During small-group activity time, Ms. G. helps children with a picture sort that includes pictures of people and objects from their garage play. They sort the pictures into labeled columns according to beginning sounds: /m/ (e.g., *mechanic, man, map, motor*); /t/ (e.g., *tire, tank, top, taillight*); and /g/ (e.g., *gas, gallon, garden, goat*). They explore the different feel of these sounds in the different parts of their mouths. They think of other words they know that "feel" the same way.

After modeling, Ms. G. gives a small deck of picture cards for the children to sort, providing direct supervision and feedback. In addition to this guided play session, the children had many other free-play experiences during the day.

Guided play provides a middle ground where you can lead children toward new ideas, new words, new roles, and new skills. At the same time you respect what children already know and can do in creating play that is satisfying to them. This play-based approach fosters children's language capabilities, builds their vocabulary, and advances their play to more mature forms.

Encouraging the development of language is one of the primary goals of teachers of young children. Deliberate instruction that stimulates language growth and is responsive to children's language strengths and needs is crucial. When you plan for and regularly use the time-honored approaches described in this chapter, you are creating contexts for teaching and learning that help children make progress in speaking, listening, reading, and writing.

CHAPTER 6

A Day in the Life of Ms. A. and Her 18 Preschoolers

This book describes how oral **language** and early **literacy** join to prepare children for school. It is meant to inform you about your role in helping young children get a good start on *a language for life* both in school and out. We know that you have many good ideas about supporting children's talking, reading, and writing. But you also probably wonder about how to pull it all together in order to provide language-filled, print-rich learning experiences for all children every day. You want to make sure you are effectively preparing children for school. In this book we have outlined the implementation of a simple model (see Figure 2, page 3) that can help you advance children's talking, reading, and writing while they are in your program.

To show you how one preschool teacher applies this simple model, we will describe a day in Ms. A.'s public preschool class of 4-year-olds. Most, but not all, of the children in the class are showing early signs of educational need, and the group as a whole fairly represents the cultural and socioeconomic diversity of a small city. As you join us on this virtual field trip, take special note of the many instances that Ms. A. is planful, purposeful, and playful.

Before the Program Starts

Before the program starts, Ms. A. maps the Early Learning Content Standards (ELCS) (Ohio Department of Education, 2003) to her language and literacy curriculum to make sure each part of her day is meeting expectations of the early childhood profession and the state. Here is how she makes a curriculum map.

First, she creates a sheet that provides a shorthand code for the performance indicators of each English language arts standard that serve as the early learning standards in her state as a quick reference (see examples in Figure 25). For example, she uses *PA* to represent the nine indicators of Standard One: Phonemic Awareness, Word Recognition and Fluency; *V* for

Figure 25
Examples of Quick Reference to Early Learning Standards

PA   **Phonemic Awareness, Word Recognition, and Fluency**
PA 1   Identify matching sounds and recognize rhymes in familiar stories, poems, songs, and words.
PA 2   Hear sounds in words by isolating the syllables of a word using snapping, clapping, or rhythmic movement (e.g., *cat*, *ap-ple*).

V   **Acquisition of Vocabulary**
V 1   Understand the meaning of new words from context of conversations, the use of pictures that accompany text, or the use of concrete objects.

RA   **Reading Applications: Informal, Technical, Persuasive, and Literary Text**
RA 1   Use pictures and illustrations to aid comprehension.
RA 2   Retell information from informational text.

WC   **Writing Conventions**
WC 1   Print letters of own name and other meaningful words with assistance using letterlike forms and/or conventional print.

Provided by Shelley Adams, preschool teacher, Kenston Early Learning Center, Bainbridge, Ohio, USA.

those performance indicators of Standard Two: Acquisition of Vocabulary; and *C* for those in Standard Ten: Communication: Oral and Visual. Coding the performance indicators in this way, she creates an easy reference tool for identifying potential objectives.

Next, she makes a template of her lesson plan, as shown in Figure 26. For each part of her day she lists the performance indicators that will always be addressed in that activity or experience. For example, when the children go to the housekeeping play center, where they scribble-write grocery lists, pretend to read cookbooks, and read environmental print on cereal boxes and coupons, she knows that the children are making progress toward Indicator PA 8: *Recognize and read familiar words or environmental print*. And, because play presents so many opportunities for learning and using new words, the plan indicates that children are also readily engaged in meeting three of the five vocabulary expectations:

V 1: *Understand the meaning of new words from context of conversations.*

V 2: *Recognize and demonstrate an understanding of environmental print.*

V 4: *Demonstrate or orally communicate position and directional words.*

Figure 26
Lesson Plan Template

Date: Unit	Additional ELCS	
12:15–12:30		**Arrival** Books and Puzzles
12:30–1:00		**Small-Group Time** Journals Table Activity
1:00–1:25		**Language and Literacy Circle 1** Fingerplays, songs Read Daily Schedule Literacy Lesson, Shared Reading Book: _____ Question of the Day
1:25–1:35		**Snack Time**
1:35–2:15		**Center Time** Art Dramatic Play Math Writing/Language Speaking/Listening Sensory/Discovery
2:20–2:40		Recess/Music and Movement/Physical Education
2:40–2:55		**Language and Literacy Circle II**
3:00		Dismissal

Provided by Shelley Adams, preschool teacher, Kenston Early Learning Center, Bainbridge, Ohio, USA.

Last, because activities for whole- and small-group time as well as play centers change, Ms. A. adds a column into her lesson plan form labeled *ELCS*, where she can note other early learning content standards that apply to a particular lesson or activity.

The Start of the Day

As the day starts, children hang up their coats or sweaters and then proceed to unpack and sort the contents of their book bags into one of two boxes located on a table outside the preschool door. One box is labeled "Books." This is where children return the books they took home the night before. The other is labeled "Folders." Here they return their home folder, which is one way Ms. A. stays in close communication with parents and caregivers. Ms. A. is particularly pleased to see that Mina, who has recently arrived from Morocco, is able to put her books in the "Books" box and her folder in the "Folders" box. Having this routine to follow seems to have made Mina more comfortable in the classroom.

Finally the bustling children sign in before entering the room, letting everyone know "I'm here today!" For Ms. A. and her teaching assistant, Ms. B., the daily routine of signing in provides an important source of ongoing assessment. Mina's mother showed Ms. A. how to write Mina's name in Arabic. Ms. A. placed Mina's name in Arabic and in English over her cubby. Now Mina is working on writing her name using the English alphabet.

Ms. A. starts with children's names rather than a letter of the week because a child's own name is extremely important at this point. Moreover, if James knows that *J* is the first letter in his name, he might recognize it somewhere else in the preschool learning environment—on the felt board, in a book, on a chart, or in another child's name printed neatly on a cubby. Ms. A. purposefully watches for children's letter recognition in an abundance of letter-naming activities that center on first letters in children's names. From these activities, all the children learn one another's names and the first letter that starts each. At the same time, these activities give the children the opportunity to play with the sound that a letter makes, to feel it with their mouths and tongues, and to think of other words (real or made up) that also start with the same sound.

Inside the Room With Books and Puzzles

After signing in, the children move to tables and browse books or put puzzles together until all the others arrive. Easing into the day in this quietly social way gives children a chance to greet each other ("Hi Jayda, my mommy bringed me today. Did you know?"), share happenings ("My Auntie JoJo is comin' for a real long time. She lives in Chicago, you know."), discuss what they see in the books they're reading ("Hey, Alex. Is this a dinosaur? Is this a pterodactyl?"), or work together to assemble a puzzle ("These is easy for us, right? Everythin's easy for us."). Ms. A. uses this time, too, to casually converse with the children one-on-one. When she stops at the table where Mina is working on a puzzle, she crouches down and says, "I see you have a puzzle, Mina. There are dogs and cats and mice and birds in your puzzle" (pointing to each type of animal as she names them). Although Mina does not say anything to Ms. A., she watches her teacher's face intently as Ms. A. names the puzzle pieces. After Ms. A. leaves, Mina says some of the words softly to herself: "Dog, bird...."

Into Small Groups

With all present and accounted for, Ms. A. then divides the children into two groups based on their individual needs. This is so she can engage them in activities that help them learn—activities that are at the appropriate level of difficulty so that with her support the children will use new skills, new words, and new ideas. One group follows Ms. B. to a table activity that provides plenty of practice in talking, reading, and writing. (See Figure 27 for a list of more table activities.)

Another group gathers around Ms. A. for a turn at journal writing, which exercises a number of early language and literacy skills directly linked to early learning objectives, such as generating ideas for a story (WP 1), hearing sounds in words (PA 2), and forming alphabet letters (WC 2). Children draw and/or write on a page that is put into their very own three-ring binder.

Figure 27
Examples of Table Activities

- Following simple oral directions to sort, order, or classify objects by one attribute
- Retelling or reenacting stories and nursery rhymes using props, magnetboards, or flannelboard pieces
- Working together to assemble a floor puzzle that focuses on the current theme
- Investigating and discussing findings about a topic of common interest to the group using books and the computer to gather information
- Making journal entries
- Participating in a new center activity; asking questions about the names and uses of new tools, objects, and materials
- Fine-motor exercises, such as cutting and pasting simple activity sheets
- Prewriting activities, such as tracing straight, wavy, and zigzag lines from left to right and completing shapes or patterns, using markers or colored pencils

Provided by Shelley Adams, preschool teacher, Kenston Early Learning Center, Bainbridge, Ohio, USA.

Today, as in the preceding months, Ms. A. gives the children a topic to draw and write about: their family, a best friend, or the caterpillars at the science table. She encourages them to take their time, to talk while they draw, and to write about their drawing in their journals. The children "read" their words to her. She writes what they say on the page and then reads it back to them with much expression. When it is Mina's turn to share her drawing, she holds it up to the group and Ms. A. comments, "What a nice job you did, Mina. Good work." Soon she will invite the children to choose their own topics. She knows some children will be ready for this step before others—while encouraging imagination and creativity on the part of all, she will still offer topics for those children who struggle to come up with their own.

After about 10 minutes, the lively groups switch so every child has a chance to join in and practice the focus activities of the day.

And Now It's Circle Time

Clap, clap, sing, song, snap, snap, chant.... Circle Time opens with songs, rhymes, and fingerplays. Ms. A. introduces a new rhyme every week, but soon the children beg to open with their favorites every day—just for the sheer delight of saying or singing the words and hearing the tinkling sounds. Ms. A., however, is quite deliberate about using this momentary silliness and fun with songs, chants, and rhymes to build the **phonological awareness** of her preschoolers. She knows that their active engagement in singing, rhyming, and chanting helps them learn to listen on purpose for the sounds in language. Last week during Circle Time, Ms. A. noticed that Mina was joining in the rhymes for the first time. In fact, this was the first time that Ms. A. had heard Mina's voice in the classroom. Today, Mina wears a big smile as she shouts out the chants with the rest of the class.

After a warm-up activity, the Schedule Reader points to each event on the day's schedule while the rest of the group reads along. As they go, Ms. A. guides them to vary their volume as they chorally read, sometimes soft as snowflakes falling to the ground and sometimes loud like drums in a parade. The children are eager to explore the sounds of their own voices along with the printed words of the schedule.

The children settle and Ms. A. begins the shared reading session. The book today is *Curious George* (Rey, 1941), an engaging tale about a mischievous monkey. Before reading, she arouses the children's interest in the story and points out the particulars of title, author, and illustrator. She takes a picture walk through the story, pointing out the illustrations, highlighting key points and interesting new words. Then she reads, and as she goes she progressively engages the children. "What do you think will happen? How do you know that? This word is *curious*. It means to be very interested in something. Isn't that a funny word? Look at how it looks, so long with so many letters in it. Did I see an *s* in there by any chance? I'm a bit worried about George. How do you feel? Well, now, wasn't that a great story? It reminds me of our field trip to the zoo a while back where we saw monkeys scampering and playing. What does it remind you of?"

"Before we leave this story, today," says Ms. A., "let's do a picture walk again. This time you help me out and we can retell this marvelous story." On another day, Ms. A. will use a different after-reading activity, such as building vocabulary, reconstructing the story with sequence cards, reviewing the rhyming words in the book, or beginning a letter- or word-matching activity.

Ms. A. consciously varies the kinds of books she reads to the children. Sometimes selections are stories and old favorites. The group adores *Lilly's Purple Plastic Purse* (Henkes, 1996) and *The Napping House* (Wood, 1984). Other times she uses informational books that boost vocabulary and basic concepts, such as *Cats* (Gibbons, 1996), *Ducks Don't Get Wet* (Goldin, 1999), and *Spiders* (Resnick, 1996). To help children remember new words, she regularly discusses them with the children after reading. She has them dramatize informational books to help them remember ideas, terms, and facts.

Circle Time draws to a close with the Question of the Day: "Did you enjoy yesterday's program with Max the Moose?" The children respond with a resounding "Yes!" They then take turns bringing up a clothespin labeled with their name and attaching it to the Yes side of the chart. However, the results for yesterday's question, "Do you like chocolate milk?" were not unanimous, with 15 "Yes" votes and a surprising 6 "No" votes. As children post their vote, they slide their finger under *Yes* or *No* as they say it. Today, for the first time, Mina not only places her name on the chart but also says the word aloud: "Yes!" With Ms. A.'s assistance, the children discuss today's results, which involves much talk and saying the word *unanimous*.

A Break for Snack

The busy children assemble for snack time. Today, like every day, Ms. A. and Ms. B. set out the snack with a sign that tells "How Many" snack items each child should count out and enjoy. The numeral is clearly written followed by dots that children can count. The teachers are deliberately building children's math skills by handling snack time in this way. Counting to 10 in the context of daily activities, touching objects and saying the number names when counting in the context of daily activities, identifying and naming numerals, and demonstrating a one-to-one correspondence when counting are important math early learning content standards addressed during this simple snack-counting routine.

Conversations abound as the teachers pose questions about the snack ("These baby carrots are crunchy, don't you think?"), prompt the sharing of preferences or similar foods served at home ("Elijah, you were telling me once that your grandma makes the best carrot cake. Is that right?"), and talk about what play centers the children plan on playing in today ("I was wondering, Rosa and Spencer, if you were planning to be garage mechanics again today. You fixed a lot of cars the other day! Mina, will you play in the House [she point to that center] today?).

On to Play for More Learning

The children huddle around Ms. A. and Ms. B. to share their play plans. They use the Play Center Chart (see Figure 28) to remind them where they played yesterday and to decide where they will start for the day.

Several boys say they want to play in the block area, but Ms. A. reminds them that they have played there a lot, so maybe today they should try a new center. "How about the sand table where you can practice making wide roads and tunnels with your bulldozers and dump trucks?" She turns to a few girls, encouraging them to think about the art area where they can make illustrations for the class *Big Recipe Book for Little Kids*. Ms. B. nods to Savannah. "Thank you, Savannah, for helping Mina choose the housekeeping area today." As the children finalize their decisions, they put their names by the center of their choice.

Savannah, Jayda, Mina, and Kennedy head off for dramatic play in the housekeeping center, which is set up to further the group's current theme of "Healthy You, Healthy Me." Cookbooks, notepads, coupons, and writing tools are available for play scenarios about cooking, food groups, and healthy eating. Ms. A. knows that the imaginative talk that goes on here develops children's use of **decontextualized** language and provides opportunities for them to use new words, such as *proteins* and *calories*. For the play to unfold, the children must listen to each other. As the children play, they are exposed to the culture, customs, and background knowledge of

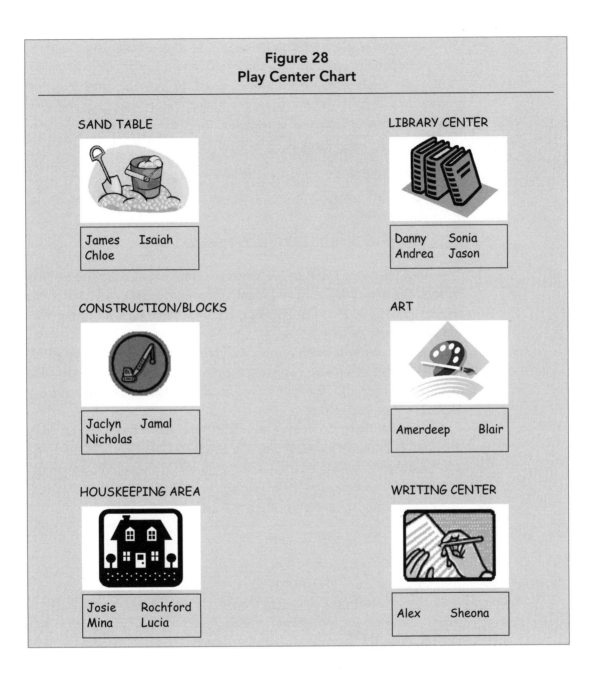

Figure 28
Play Center Chart

SAND TABLE

James   Isaiah
Chloe

LIBRARY CENTER

Danny   Sonia
Andrea   Jason

CONSTRUCTION/BLOCKS

Jaclyn   Jamal
Nicholas

ART

Amerdeep   Blair

HOUSKEEPING AREA

Josie   Rochford
Mina   Lucia

WRITING CENTER

Alex   Sheona

their friends. Although Mina does not add any talk to the play, she is a willing participant and listens carefully to the other children as they develop their play themes.

One trio beelines for the block/truck construction area where there are all kinds of books on construction as well as paper and pencils to take work orders and a set of blueprints to refer to. Another moves toward the writing center stocked with all manner of writing supplies such as stencils, pens, pencils, envelopes, tactile letters, and different kinds of paper. Other materials are purposefully placed to provide practice with recognizing alphabet letters, making writing attempts, matching and sorting sounds, and other activities related to this week's objectives:

- use new, topic-related words during play
- express ideas through drawing and writing
- play and manipulate sounds in words by saying and pronouncing and sorting
- recognize alphabet letters in own name

One foursome heads to the language center because they like to play school. Today they will read and manipulate several interactive charts (see Figure 29). "Little Miss Muffet" is especially popular because of that awful, scary word, *spider*.

After a few squeamish rounds with the word *spider*, the group splits, with some children inserting picture cards of other creatures into the Miss Muffet chart and others exploring different charts with familiar nursery rhymes, songs, and chants.

Ms. A. and Ms. B. circulate among the play centers with several goals in mind. They model language and play behaviors. They support children's efforts and play along at their direction. And, while the children are deeply immersed in the flow of play, the teachers quietly and unobtrusively assess their use of language and early literacy skills.

Figure 29
Interactive Poem Chart

Little Miss Muffet sat on a tuffet
Eating her curds and whey,
Along came a
And sat down beside her,
And frightened Miss Muffet away!

Bringing an end to center play, Ms. A. and Ms. B lead the children out the door to the playground for some time in the sunshine. They introduce a game—Duck, Duck, Goose—to the children. Ms. A. is pleased to see that Mina is an active participant in this game, as it had been difficult at first getting her involved in games. But today she is as eager as the other children to take her turn, touching each child and saying "Duck," until she comes to the one she wants to pick as the "Goose." After a few rounds, Ms. A. asks Jared to give the directions, which he does with a great voice of authority. And everybody follows along except Rosa, who is busy with her left shoe.

The Close of the Day

The children gather together and Ms. A. passes around the Mystery Box. "So, what do you think it is? What does it feel like? Tell me some more. Savannah said it felt like it had *ridges*. What do you think she meant?"

The children feel and talk. "It feels like a round thing. Does it go on our trucks? It has hard spots." They listen intently for more clues. All the while, Ms. A. knows that she is helping the children learn to listen, to use descriptive words, and to express their thinking with language. She continues to encourage talk for a short bit and then turns to the easel for shared writing. "Let's record this mystery," she says, and she begins to write what the children have to say. Alex says, "It feels like a round thing." Ms. A. talks about the words as she writes, "*It* is a short word and I hear a /t/ at the end. I need to leave a space before I start to write *feels*." She finishes the sentence and then takes another. After three or four sentences, the children have enough clues to identify the mystery object—a small tire that fell off one of the tractors in the block area. "We were looking for that tire, Ms. A." Missing object found and mystery solved!

At the completion of this whole-group time, children choose take-home books, get their mail, and then go to their cubbies and pack their backpacks for dismissal.

As the Program Goes

To assess children's progress and the everyday effectiveness of their program, Ms. A. and Ms. B. keep anecdotal records in addition to more formal assessments (e.g., *Peabody Picture Vocabulary Test*). Using a clipboard, they record observations on small sticky notes every day. Their notes may consist of observations, such as noting the day Isaiah wrote the letter *I* for the first time, or a child's accomplishments related to a performance indicator (e.g., *Speaks clearly and understandably.* Elijah 9-5-03 "This chicken." 9-25-03 "This a chicken leg."). These observational notes are later transferred to a child language and literacy portfolio or binder that is divided into six sections: Oral Language Comprehension, Vocabulary, Alphabet Letter Knowledge, Phonological Awareness, Concepts About Print, and Writing.

From these daily entries, individual patterns of progress are determined in each skill area and considered in light of research-based learning trajectories and early learning **standards**. When meeting with parents and colleagues regarding a child's growth, these notes provide critical information for communicating specific strengths and needs.

We appreciate the opportunity to visit Ms. A. and her 18 preschoolers, if only for a short time. We learn from her example that preschool teachers can join oral language and early literacy in their settings to help children learn language, learn about language, and learn through language. Guided by early learning expectations in language and literacy, they can be planful. Deliberate in their choices of activities, they can be purposeful. And genuinely active in their teaching role, they become playful. As a result all young children grow more capable in their abilities to talk, read, and write—and to flourish in school.

Easy-to-Use Language and Literacy Assessment Tools

Get Ready to Read (Pearson Education, 2001)
www.getreadytoread.org
888-575-7373

Book Buddies Early Literacy Screening (Guilford, 1998)
http://curry.edschool.virginia.edu/reading/projects/bookbuddies/home.html
804-662-7464

Test of Early Reading Ability: 3 (PRO-ED, 2001)
Test of Oral Language Development (TOLD) (PRO-ED, 1998)
www.proedinc.com
800-897-3202

Doors to Discovery Assessment Handbook (Wright Group/McGraw-Hill, 2002)
www.wrightgroup.com
800-648-2970

PALS PreK: Phonological Awareness Literacy Screening for Preschool
(University of Virginia Press, 2002)
http://pals.virginia.edu/default.asp
800-882-7257

Principles of Program Evaluation

- The aim of evaluation is to engage in continuous improvement. Regular evaluation is necessary to find out how well a program is achieving results.
- Evaluation is guided by program goals. The design and tools of evaluation address these goals.
- Evaluation uses appropriate, valid, and reliable child outcome data to determine program effectiveness.
- Evaluation is conducted by well-trained individuals who are knowledgeable of program evaluation procedures and ethics.
- Evaluation involves relevant others, such as families. It is the basis for program improvement and results in change over time.

Adapted from *National Association for the Education of Young Children/National Association of Early Childhood Specialists in State Departments of Education (NAEYC/NAECS/SDE) Joint Position Statement on Early Childhood Curriculum, Assessment and Program Evaluation* (2003)

Daily Language and Literacy Routines for Infants and Toddlers

A dults who care for young children can start them early on the road to school success. What adults know and do has a tremendous influence on children's language and beginning literacy. Talking a lot with young children, reciting nursery rhymes, reading storybooks, telling tales, handing down oral stories from days gone by—these are simple ways that adults can help babies and toddlers learn language and begin with books. Every adult should know about and practice the following daily routines with the young children they care for and care about.

Daily Routine I: Cooing and Connecting With Infants and Toddlers

Adults should know:

Singing, talking, and reading to infants and toddlers is very important. When adults coo, sing, talk, and read aloud, babies and toddlers look and listen. They are learning language.

Adults should do this:

• Talk about what you are doing in the course of daily care, such as feeding, potty/diapering, and putting children to bed.

> "Daddy is washing your hands before we eat so they will be clean. See, we're washing the dirt and germs away."
>
> "Grandma is changing your diaper because it is very wet and she wants to keep you dry and comfortable."
>
> "Let's take off your shoes and socks before you go to bed. This little piggy went to the market...This little piggy..."

From Mary P. White, Cuyahoga Community College Early Literacy Mentor Project, Cleveland, Ohio, USA.

- Imitate baby's cooing and babbling so as to respond to his or her first attempts at conversation.

- Set aside time for storybook reading everyday. Mark it on the calendar.

Daily Routine II: Talking With Ones, Twos, and Threes

Adults should know:

They are the best suppliers of words to children. When they talk to children, they are helping them to build up a store of words they can use right now to express themselves and later on to aid reading comprehension.

Adults should do this:

- Listen attentively and respond to children when they are talking.

> "That's so interesting. Tell me more about your trip to the Health Museum."
>
> "I don't know much about building rockets. What did you learn when you were watching the rocket video?"
>
> "What happened next?"
>
> "Why did you like that story?"
>
> "What are some fun things that you would like to do for your birthday party?"

- Use new words when conversing with children.

> "I'm famished. Let's stop for some pizza."
>
> "That dog is a stray dog because he is roaming around without a leash."
>
> "It seems as if you were having fun on the playground. Everyone started to grumble when it was time to come in."

• Read quality books that tell stories and provide information.

• Supply props for play, i.e. puppets, tools, dress-up clothes, paper, markers and pens, along with fascinating objects, such as sea shells, feathers, magnets, magnifying glasses, keys.

Daily Routine III: Storybook Reading With Ones, Twos, and Threes

Adults should know:

The single most important activity for nurturing learning in children is to read quality books to them. When you read to children using shared reading techniques, you help them learn new ideas and new words. Shared storybook reading means that the children help you read and talk about the book.

Adults should do this:

• Read 3–5 quality books to children everyday.

• Reread children's favorite books to them.

• *Before reading*, point out the author and guess what the book might be about

• *During reading*, stop and talk about the illustrations, the story line, and personal thoughts and feelings.

• *After reading*, remember favorite parts together.

Daily Routine IV: Playing With the Sounds of Language

Adults should know:

Children need to learn to pay attention to the sounds they hear in words. Eventually they must learn to match sounds to letters. Children need adults' help to learn this skill.

Adults should do this:

- Recite traditional nursery rhymes often.

> Peter, Peter, pumpkin eater / Had a wife and couldn't keep her;
> So he put her in a pumpkin shell / And there he kept her very well.

- Recite nursery rhymes with some body motions.

> London Bridge Is Falling Down
> Ring Around the Rosy
> I'm a Little Teapot
> Here We Go Round the Mulberry Bush
> This Is the Way We Wash Our Clothes

- Encourage children to make up their own rhymes and alliteration.

> Willaby, Wallaby, Wee an elephant sat on me.
> Willaby, Wallaby, Woo an elephant sat on you.
> Willaby, Wallaby, Waddie, an elephant sat on Maddie.
> Willaby, Wallaby, Wickie, an elephant sat on Rickey.

- Read rhyming books to children.

> *Two Shoes, New Shoes* (Shirley Hughes)
> *Chicken Soup With Rice* (Maurice Sendak)
> *Hop on Pop* (Dr. Seuss)
> *The Mouse That Snored* (Bernard Waber)
> *Silly Sally* (Audrey Wood)

Daily Routine V: Playing With the Alphabet

Adults should know:

Children need to learn to recognize the alphabet letters. The best way to teach the alphabet is to help children learn the letters of their own name and those of a few common words in everyday life, for example, *hello, welcome, love, stop.*

Adults should do this:

• Talk about letters and words that surround us at home and in the community.

• Make home and school settings abundant with print.

• Make markers, pencils, and paper available for drawing and writing.

• Write in front of children and explain what you are doing.

• Encourage children to draw, scribble, and write letters and words.

• Provide alphabet games, magnetic letters, and alphabet puzzles.

• Point out familiar signs outdoors: traffic signs, billboards, fast food restaurant signs, and yard signs.

When families and caregivers put daily routines like these into practice, they help very young children grow and thrive as language learners. The benefits of singing, playing with words, conversing with and reading to children are truly immeasurable—not only in helping children learn language, but also in bringing joy and laughter to family life.

REFERENCES

Biemiller, A., & Slonim, N. (2001). Estimating root word vocabulary growth in normative and advantaged populations: Evidence for a common sequence of vocabulary acquisition. *Journal of Educational Psychology, 93,* 498–520.

Bloom, P. (2000). *How children learn the meanings of words.* Cambridge, MA: MIT Press.

Bodrova, E., & Leong, D.J. (1996). *Tools of the mind: A Vygotskian approach to early childhood education.* Englewood Cliffs, NJ: Prentice Hall.

Bowman, B.T., Donovan, S., & Burns, M.S. (2001). *Eager to learn: Educating our preschoolers.* Washington, DC: National Academy Press.

Breneman, L.N., & Breneman, B. (1983). *Once upon a time: A storytelling handbook.* Chicago: Nelson-Hall.

Chall, J. (1983). *Stages of reading development.* New York: McGraw-Hill.

Chall, J. (1996). *Stages of reading development* (2nd ed.). Fort Worth, TX: Harcourt College.

Crystal, D. (1992). *An encyclopedia dictionary of language and languages.* London: Penguin.

Daniels, H., & Zemelman, S. (1985). *A writing project: Training teachers of composition from kindergarten to college.* Portsmouth, NH: Heinemann.

Doors to Discovery Assessment Handbook. (2002). Bothell, WA: Wright Group/ McGraw-Hill.

Dunn, L.M., Dunn, L.M., Robertson, G.J., & Eisenberg, J.L. (1997). *Peabody Picture Vocabulary Test* (3rd ed.). Circle Pines, MN: American Guidance Service.

Gunnewig, S., & McGloin, D. (2003). *Online professional development in early literacy.* New York: Teachscape.

Halliday, M.A.K. (1977). *Learning how to mean: Explorations in the development of language.* New York: Reed Elsevier.

International Reading Association & National Association for the Education of Young Children. (1998). *Learning to read and write: Developmentally appropriate practices for young children.* Newark, DE: Author; Washington, DC: Author.

Mardell, B. (1999). *From basketball to the Beatles: In search of compelling early childhood curriculum.* Portsmouth, NH: Heinemann.

McGee, L.M., & Richgels, D.J. (2003). *Designing early literacy programs: Strategies for at-risk preschool and kindergarten children.* New York: Guilford.

McLaughlin, B., Blanchard, A.G., & Osanai, Y. (1995). *Assessing language development in bilingual preschool children.* Washington, DC: National Clearinghouse for Bilingual Education. Retrieved March 25, 2004, from http://www.ncela.gwu.edu/ ncbepubs/pigs/pig22.htm

Neuman, S.B., & Roskos, K.A. (1989). Preschoolers' conceptions of literacy as reflected in their spontaneous play. In S. McCormick, J. Zutell, P. Scharer, & P.R. Okeefe (Eds.), *Cognitive and social perspectives for literacy research and instruction*

(38th yearbook of the National Reading Conference, pp. 87–94). Chicago: National Reading Conference.

Ohio Department of Education. (2003). *Early Learning Content Standards.* Retrieved May 17, 2004, from http://www.ode.ste.oh.us/ece/pdf/ELCS.pdf

Roskos, K.A., Christie, J.F., & Richgels, D.J. (2003). The essentials of early literacy instruction. *Young Children, 58*(2), 52–60.

Saville-Troike, M. (1987). Dilingual discourse: The negotiation of meaning without a common code. *Linguistics, 25*, 81–106.

Shonkoff, J.P., & Phillips, D.A. (Eds.). (2000). *From neurons to neighborhoods: The science of early child development.* Washington, DC: National Academy Press.

Snow, C., Burns, M.S., & Griffin, P. (Eds.). (1998). *Preventing reading difficulties in young children.* Washington, DC: National Academy Press.

Soderman, A.K., Gregory, K.M., & O'Neill, L.T. (1999). *Scaffolding emergent literacy: A child-centered approach for preschool through grade 5.* Boston: Allyn & Bacon.

Stanovich, K.E. (2000). *Progress in understanding reading: Scientific foundations and new frontiers.* New York: Guilford.

U.S. Department of Health and Human Services. (2003). *The Head Start path to positive child outcomes.* [The Head Start Child Outcomes Framework] Retrieved May 18, 2004, from http://www.hsnrc.org/CDI/outcontent.cfm

Vukelich, C., Christie, J., & Enz, B. (2002). *Helping young children learn language and literacy.* Boston: Allyn & Bacon.

Wong Fillmore, L. (1979). Individual differences in second language acquisition. In C.J. Fillmore, D. Kempler, & W. Wang (Eds.), *Individual differences in language ability and language behavior* (pp. 203–228). New York: Academic.

CHILDREN'S LITERATURE CITED

Gibbons, G. (1996). *Cats.* New York: Scholastic.

Goldin, A. (1965). *Ducks don't get wet.* Toronto: Fitzhenry & Whiteside Limited.

Henkes, K. (1996). *Lilly's purple plastic purse.* New York: Greenwillow.

Hughes, S. (1996). *Two shoes, new shoes.* New York: HarperCollins.

Lee, D. (2002). *Sylvia's garage.* Bothell, WA: Wright Group.

Nicholas, E. (1992). *Knock it down, build it up!* Bothell, WA: Wright Group.

Resnick, J.P. (1996). *Eyes on nature: Spiders.* Chicago: Kidsbooks.

Rey, H.A. (1941). *Curious George.* Boston: Houghton Mifflin.

Rotner, S., & Kelly, S.M. (1996). *Lots of moms.* New York: Dial.

Rotner, S., & Kelly, S.M. (1997). *Lots of dads.* New York: Dial.

Sendak, M. (1962). *Chicken soup with rice.* New York: HarperCollins.

Seuss, Dr. (1963). *Hop on pop.* New York: Random House.

Waber, B. (2000). *The mouse that snored.* Boston: Houghton Mifflin.

Williams, R.L. (2002). *Families share.* Huntington Beach, CA: Creative Teaching Press.

Wood, A. (1984). *The napping house.* San Diego: Harcourt.

Wood, A. (1992). *Silly Sally.* San Diego: Harcourt Trade.

INDEX

Note: Page numbers followed by *f* indicate figures.

A

ACTIVITY TIME, 25–26
ADAMS, SHELLEY, 70*f*, 71*f*, 73*f*
ADULTS: as resources, 30
ALPHABET KNOWLEDGE, 3; assessment of, 21, 21*f*; definition of, vii, 6; for infants and toddlers, 89
ASSESSMENT: chart for, 21*f*; daily input on, 79–80; and planning, 18–22; tools for, 81

B

BIEMILLER, A., 23
BLANCHARD, A.G., 18
BLOOM, P., 10
BODROVA, E., 28*f*, 40
BOOKS: in classroom, 72–73; evaluation checklist for, 32*f*
BOWMAN, B.T., 4, 43
BRENEMAN, B., 54*f*
BRENEMAN, L.N., 54*f*
BURNS, M.S., 1, 4, 7, 41, 43

C

CALENDAR: wall, for daily news, 44–45
CHALL, J., 7*f*
CHARTS: assessment, 21*f*; pocket, 44; poem, interactive, 78, 78*f*
CHRISTIE, J.F., 6*f*, 66
CIRCLE TIME, 26, 74–75
CLASSROOM: entering, 72–73
CLOSE: of day, 79
COMMUNICATION, 5; definition of, vii, 6; shared writing and, 60
COMPLETION PROMPTS, 43
CONCEPTS OF PRINT. *See* print knowledge
CONVERSATION: everyday, 35–36; at snack time, 76; stretchers for, 37*f*
CROWD PROMPTS, 43–44
CRYSTAL, D., vii
CURRICULUM MAP, 69–71

D

DAILY PLAN, 25–27; essentials in, 27–33; sample, 31*f*
DAILY ROUTINES: language and literacy, for infants and toddlers, 85–89

DANIELS, H., 53

DAY: close of, 79; start of, 25–26, 71–73

DECONTEXTUALIZED LANGUAGE: definition of, vii; in play, 76; print as, 11; speech as, 26; storytelling as, 54

DEPARTMENT OF EDUCATION, 16f

DIALOGIC READING, 42–44

DISTANCING PROMPTS, 44

DONOVAN, S., 4, 43

DOORS TO DISCOVERY ASSESSMENT HANDBOOK, 20f

DUNN, L.M., 21–22

E–F

EARLY LITERACY: concepts of, 5–13; day of instruction in, 69–80; functions in, 11f; instructional approaches to, 49–67; oral language and, 1–4, 3f; standards in, sources of, 16f

EARLY LITERACY LEARNING: planning for, 15–33

EISENBERG, J.L., 21

ENGLISH-LANGUAGE LEARNERS. *See* second-language development

ENZ, B., 6f

EVALUATION, 21–22; definition of, vii; program, principles of, 83

EVERYDAY CONVERSATION, 35–36

EXPRESSIVE LANGUAGE: definition of, vii

EXPRESSIVE VOCABULARY, 10

FAMILY: daily language and literacy routines for, 85–89

G

GAMES: with names, 47

GIBBONS, G., 75

GOALS: and objectives, 16, 16f

GOLDIN, A., 75

GREETING TIME, 25

GREGORY, K.M., 41

GRIFFIN, P., 1, 7, 41

GUIDED PARTICIPATION, 38–40; framework for, 39f

GUIDED PLAY: as instructional approach, 64–67

GUNNEWIG, S., 1

H

HALLIDAY, M.A.K., 10–11, 11f

HEAD START CHILD OUTCOMES FRAMEWORK, 15, 16f; on phonological awareness, 51f

HENKES, K., 75

HUGHES, S., 88

I–K

INFANTS: daily language and literacy routines for, 85–89

INSTRUCTIONAL APPROACHES, 36–38, 49–50; to oral language and early literacy, 49–67

INTERACTIVE POEM CHART, 78, 78*f*
INTERNATIONAL READING ASSOCIATION (IRA), 15
INVITATIONS: writing, 61
JOURNAL WRITING, 73–74
KELLY, S.M., 63

L

LANGUAGE, 2, 15; daily routines for toddlers, 85–89; definition of, vii, 6; early learning, standards in, sources of, 16*f*; functions of, 11*f*; scaffolds for, 40–41
LANGUAGE DEVELOPMENT, 5; milestones in, 6*f*
LANGUAGE EXPERIENCE APPROACH (LEA), 42, 43*f*
LANGUAGE LEARNING: approaches to, 1–2
LEARNING CONDITIONS: creating, 35–48; definition of, 35
LEARNING TRAJECTORIES, 22–24, 23*f*
LEE, D., 66
LEONG, D.J., 28*f*, 40
LESSON PLANS: template of, 70, 71*f*
LESSONS: with guided play, 66–67; with shared reading, 58–59; with shared writing, 61; with show and tell, 63–64; with singing and rhyming, 52–53; with storytelling, 55–56
LISTENING: skills in, 12–13
LITERACY, 2; daily routines for toddlers, 85–89; definition of, v, vii, 7
LONG-TERM PLAN, 15–16; development of, 22–24; weekly planner and, 25–27

M

MARDELL, B., 30
MCGEE, L.M., 26*f*
MCGLOIN, D., 1
MCLAUGHLIN, B., 18
MCREL FRAMEWORK FOR EARLY LITERACY INSTRUCTION, 16*f*
METALINGUISTIC AWARENESS: definition of, vii
MONITORING, 21; definition of, vii

N

NAMES: games with, 47; sign-in procedure and, 25, 26*f*
NATIONAL ASSOCIATION FOR THE EDUCATION OF YOUNG CHILDREN (NAEYC), 15
NEUMAN, S.B., 10–11, 11*f*
NICHOLAS, E., 17
NURSERY RHYMES, 45–46

O

OBJECTIVES: goals and, 16, 16*f*
OHIO DEPARTMENT OF EDUCATION, 69
O'NEILL, L.T., 41
OPEN-ENDED PROMPTS, 43–44

ORAL LANGUAGE: checklist for, 20*f*; concepts of, 5–13; day of instruction in, 69–80; definition of, v; and early literacy, 1–4, 3*f*; instructional approaches to, 49–67; planning for, 15–33

ORAL LANGUAGE COMPREHENSION, 3; assessment of, 21, 21*f*; definition of, vii, 8

OSANAI, Y., 18

OUTDOOR TIME, 27

P–Q

PARENTS: daily language and literacy routines for, 85–89

PARTICIPATION: guided, 38–40; framework for, 39*f*

PHILLIPS, D.A., 4, 41

PHONOLOGICAL AWARENESS, 3, 13; assessment of, 21, 21*f*; definition of, vii, 8–9; standards on, 51*f*

PLANFULNESS, 1, 2*f*

PLANNING, 15–33; daily, 25–33; long-term, 15–16, 22–24; for play, 41–42; short-term, 16–17

PLAY: characteristics of, by end of kindergarten, 28*f*; in classroom, 76–79; guided, as instructional approach, 64–67; with infants and toddlers, 87–89; planning for, 41–42; with sounds and words, 50*f*; standards for, 28–30

PLAY CENTER BOARD, 29, 29*f*, 76, 77*f*

PLAYFULNESS, 1, 2*f*

POCKET CHARTS, 44

POEMS: interactive chart, 78, 78*f*

PRACTICE, 41–47

PREDICTIONS: making, 12

PRINT: relation to talk, 10–12

PRINT KNOWLEDGE: assessment of, 21, 21*f*; definition of, vii

PROGRAM EVALUATION: principles of, 83

PROMPTS: CROWD, 43–44

PURPOSEFULNESS, 1, 2*f*

PUZZLES: in classroom, 72–73

QUESTIONS: asking and answering, 12; what/where/when/why, 43

R

READING: dialogic, 42–44; with infants and toddlers, 87; learning conditions for, 35–48; planning for, 15–33; shared, as instructional approach, 56–59; skills in, 12–13

READING DEVELOPMENT: early stages of, 7*f*

RECALL PROMPTS, 43

RECEPTIVE LANGUAGE: definition of, viii

RECEPTIVE VOCABULARY, 10

RESNICK, J.P., 75

RESOURCES: evaluation checklist for, 32*f*–33*f*; making the most of, 30–32

RETELLING, 12–13

REY, H.A., 74

RHYMING: as instructional approach, 50–53

RHYTHM: of day, 25–27
RICHGELS, D.J., 26*f*, 66
ROBERTSON, G.J., 21
ROSKOS, K., 10–11, 11*f*, 66
ROTNER, S., 63

S

SAVILLE-TROIKE, M., 18–19
SCAFFOLDING: definition of, viii, 40; language, 40–41
SCREENING, 19; definition of, viii
SECOND-LANGUAGE DEVELOPMENT, 5; assessment of, 18–19; in classroom, 48; story-telling and, 53
SENDAK, M., 88
SENSE OF STORY, 13
SEUSS, DR., 88
SHARED READING: as instructional approach, 56–59
SHARED WRITING: as instructional approach, 59–61
SHONKOFF, J.P., 4, 41
SHOW AND TELL: as instructional approach, 61–64
SIGNATURES: in classroom, 46–47
SIGN-IN PROCEDURE, 25, 26*f*
SINGING: as instructional approach, 50–53
SLONIM, N., 23
SMALL GROUPS, 73–74
SNACK TIME, 75–76
SNOW, C., 1, 7, 41
SODERMAN, A.K., 41
SOFTWARE: evaluation checklist for, 33*f*
SOUNDS: play with, 50*f*
SPEECH: definition of, viii, 9; skills in, 12–13
STANDARDS: definition of, viii; for early literacy and language learning, sources of, 16*f*; guided play and, 64–65; quick reference to, examples of, 70*f*; shared reading and, 56; shared writing and, 60; show and tell and, 62; singing and rhyming and, 51; storytelling and, 54; for work and play, 28–30
STANOVICH, K.E., 8
START: of day, 25–26, 71–73
STORY: selection of, 54*f*; sense of, 13
STORYTELLING: as instructional approach, 53–56; preparation for, 55

T–U

TABLE ACTIVITIES, 73, 73*f*
TALK: definition of, v, viii, 9–10; with infants and toddlers, 86–87; learning conditions for, 35–48; planning for, 15–33; relation to print, 10–12
TEACHERS: judgments by, v; qualities of, for oral language learning, 1, 2*f*
TELLING, 12–13. *See also* show and tell; storytelling
THEMATIC ORGANIZERS, 24

THEMES: extraordinary, features of, 24*f*

TODDLERS: daily language and literacy routines for, 85–89

TOYS: evaluation checklist for, 32*f*–33*f*

TWARDOSZ, SANDRA, 31*f*

U.S. DEPARTMENT OF HEALTH AND HUMAN SERVICES, 6, 15, 51*f*

V

VOCABULARY, 1; assessment of, 21, 21*f*; definition of, viii, 10

VYGOTSKY, LEV, 59

VUKELICH, C., 6*f*

W–Z

WABER, B., 88

WALL CALENDAR: for daily news, 44–45

WEBSITES: evaluation checklist for, 33*f*; for nursery rhymes, 46

WEEKLY PLANNER, 16–17, 17*f*, 25–27

WHAT/WHERE/WHEN/WHY QUESTIONS, 44

WHITE, MARY P., 85

WILLIAMS, R.L., 63

WONG FILLMORE, L., 19

WOOD, A., 75, 88

WORD PLAY, 50, 50*f*; definition of, viii

WORK: standards for, 28–30

WRITING: journals, 73–74; learning conditions for, 35–48; planning for, 15–33; shared, as instructional approach, 59–61; skills in, 12–13

ZEMELMAN, S., 53